Mathematics for credit
Book 1

Mathematics for credit
Book 1

Alan Caldow and Morag McClurg

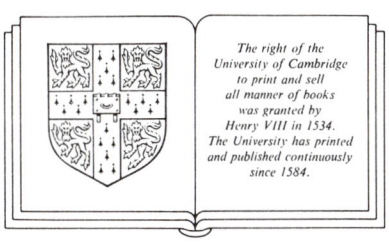

Cambridge University Press

Cambridge
New York   Port Chester
Melbourne   Sydney

Published by the Press Syndicate of the University of Cambridge
The Pitt Building, Trumpington Street, Cambridge CB2 1RP
32 East 57th Street, New York, NY 10022, USA
10 Stamford Road, Oakleigh, Melbourne 3166, Australia

© Cambridge University Press 1989

First published 1989

Diagrams and typesetting by DMD Ltd, St Clements, Oxford

Printed in Great Britain by Scotprint, Musselborough, Scotland

British Library Cataloguing in Publication Data
Caldow, Alan
  Mathematics for credit
  Bk.1
  1. Mathematics
  I. Title II. McClurg, Morag
  510
  ISBN 0–521–36900–2

Cover illustration © 1989 M. C. Escher Heirs/Cordon Art-Baarn-Holland

Contents

1	Inequations	1
	Money management 1: pay and income tax	12
2	Square roots	19
	Money management 2: index numbers	28
3	Special angles	32
	Consolidation 1	35
4	Graphs (1)	39
	Money management 3: hire purchase and VAT	61
5	Angles greater than 90°	65
	Money management 4: savings and investment	78
6	Similar triangles	83
	Consolidation 2	99
7	The cosine rule	104
	Money management 5: loans and insurance	115
8	Patterns	122
9	Variation	130
	Consolidation 3	147

1 Inequations

A Balances

Mrs Hatch had twins called Michelle and Thomas.

Michelle weighed 3 kg. Thomas weighed 2·8 kg.

If Michelle and Thomas were placed on balance scales, this would happen.

A1 Copy and complete this sentence, using > (greater than) or < (less than).

The weight of Michelle . . . the weight of Thomas.

A2 How do you know, just by looking at the balance scales, which baby is the heavier?

Each baby had a packet of nappies which weighed 2 kg. If the babies and their nappies were put on the balance scales, this would happen.

Here is how we could check this:

Weight of Michelle = 3 kg
Weight of nappies = 2 kg
Weight of Michelle + nappies = 5 kg

Weight of Thomas = 2·8 kg
Weight of nappies = 2 kg
Weight of Thomas + nappies = 4·8 kg

A3 Copy and complete this sentence, using > or <.

Weight of Michelle + nappies . . . weight of Thomas + nappies.

You should now see that

If we add the same amount to both sides, the scales are still tipped the same way.

Here are pictures of two salesmen who sell 'Corby', the amazing vacuum cleaner.

Savaas and his vacuum cleaner weigh 85 kg.

Stuart and his vacuum cleaner weigh 90 kg.

If Savaas and Stuart, with their vacuum cleaners, were placed on balance scales, this would happen.

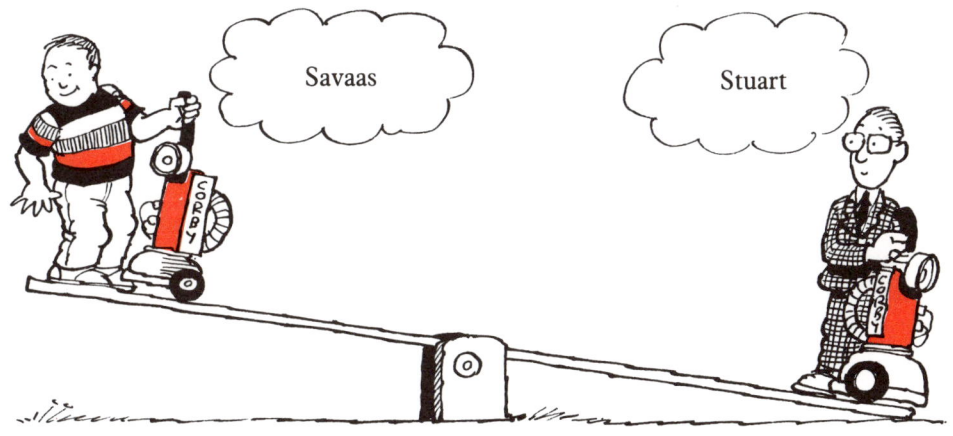

A4 Copy and complete this sentence, using > or <.

Weight of Savaas + cleaner . . . weight of Stuart + cleaner.

If they were both weighed without their vacuum cleaners, this would happen.

Here is how we could check this:

Weight of Savaas + cleaner = 85 kg		Weight of Stuart + cleaner = 90 kg	
Weight of cleaner = 8 kg		Weight of cleaner = 8 kg	
So weight of Savaas = 77 kg		So weight of Stuart = 82 kg	

A5 Copy and complete this sentence, using > or <.

Weight of Savaas . . . weight of Stuart.

Notice that

If we subtract the same amount from both sides, the scales are still tipped the same way.

B Solving simple inequations

Consider the inequation $x - 2 > 5$.

If we put $x - 2$ on one scale pan and 5 on the other, the scales would look like this.

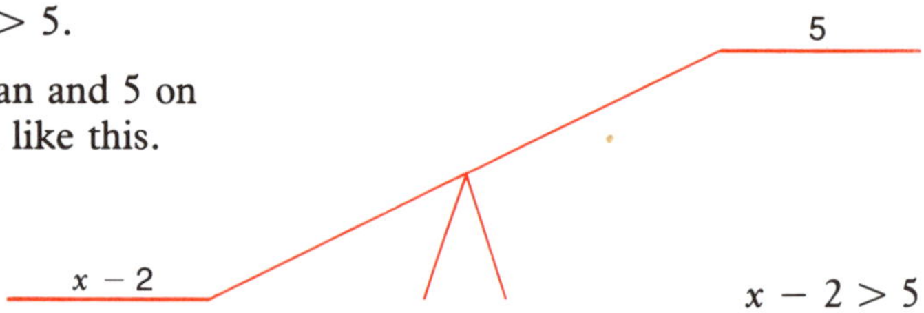

$x - 2 > 5$

Now we can add or subtract the same amount to both sides, and it will not affect the balance.

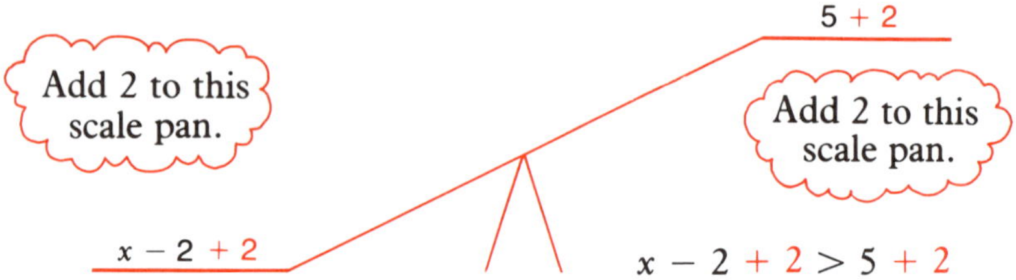

Add 2 to this scale pan.

Add 2 to this scale pan.

$x - 2 + 2 > 5 + 2$

So now we can say $\quad x - 2 + 2 > 5 + 2$
$\qquad\qquad\qquad\qquad x > 7 \qquad$ (collecting terms)

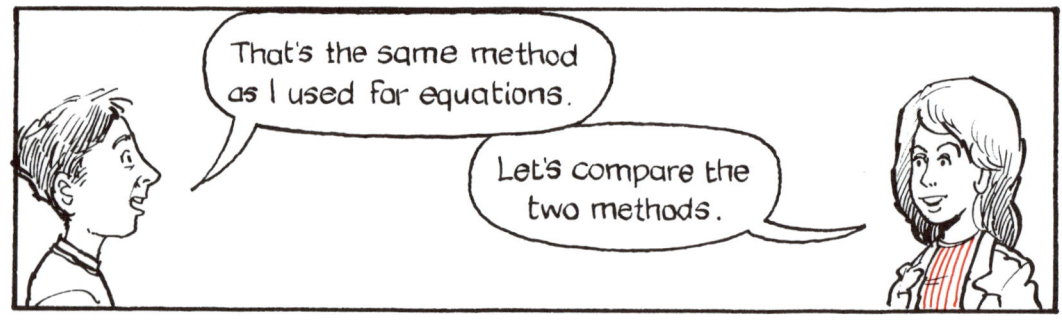

That's the same method as I used for equations.

Let's compare the two methods.

Equation		Inequation
$x - 2 = 5$	Add 2 to both sides.	$x - 2 > 5$
$x - 2 + 2 = 5 + 2$	The $+2$ and -2 cancel out.	$x - 2 + 2 > 5 + 2$
$x = 7$		$x > 7$

I wonder if that would work for $x + 7 < 11$

Of course it would because you could <u>subtract</u> 7 from both sides.

B1 Copy and complete the working for this inequation.

$$x + 7 < 11$$
$$x + 7 - 7 < 11 - \ldots$$
$$\ldots < \ldots$$

B2 Solve each of these inequations, setting out your working as in question B1.

(a) $x - 3 < 9$ (b) $x + 6 < 7$ (c) $x - 4 > 2$ (d) $x + 2 > 6$

(e) $x + 8 > 1$ (f) $x - 5 > 12$ (g) $3 + x < 7$ (h) $-1 + x > 8$

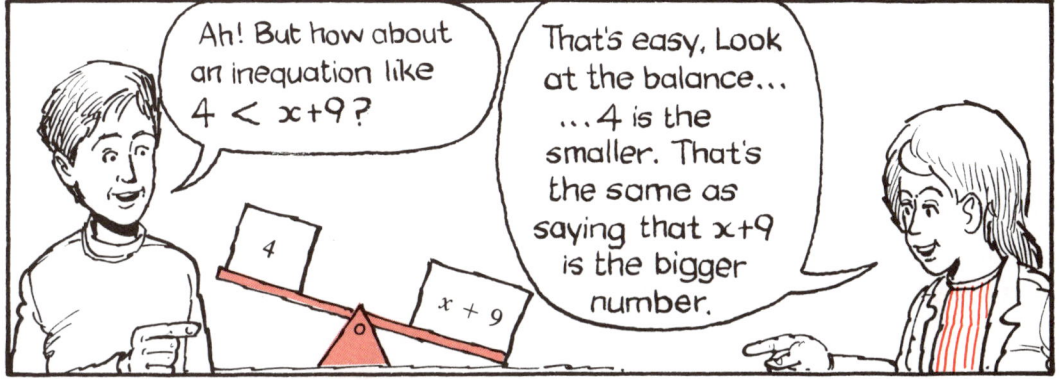

So $\quad\quad\quad\quad 4 < x + 9$
is the same as $\quad x + 9 > 4$

We can now do the same as before.

$$x + 9 - 9 > 4 - 9$$
$$x > -5$$

Subtract 9 from both sides. The +9 and −9 cancel out.

B3 Copy and complete the working for this inequation.

$$9 > x - 2$$
is the same as $\quad x - 2 < 9$
Add 2 to both sides. $\quad x - 2 + \ldots < 9 + \ldots$
$$\ldots \ldots \ldots$$
$$x \ldots \ldots$$

B4 Now solve each of these inequations.

(a) $5 < x + 1$ (b) $2 < x - 5$ (c) $6 > x + 2$ (d) $7 > x - 1$

(e) $-2 < x - 1$ (f) $4 < 7 + x$ (g) $5 > x + 8$ (h) $-6 > -2 + x$

B5 Solve each of these inequations.

(a) $x - 1 < 4$ (b) $x + 2 < 5$ (c) $x - 3 > 2$

(d) $x + 7 > -1$ (e) $1 + x > -5$ (f) $-3 + x < 2$

(g) $3 + x < -1$ (h) $4 < x + 2$ (i) $-1 > 5 + x$

(j) $16 > 3 + x$ (k) $x - 7 < 9$ (l) $3 < x - 5$

C Other 'interesting' inequations

The Bolt brothers are identical twins.

When one of them stands on the balance pan, this happens.

So   weight of one twin > 45 kg.

If both twins stood on the balance pan together, what would they weigh more than?

So   weight of two twins > 90 kg.

The conclusion we can draw from this is that

If we multiply both sides of an inequation by the same number, the balance is unchanged.

C1 Copy and complete the working for each of these inequations.

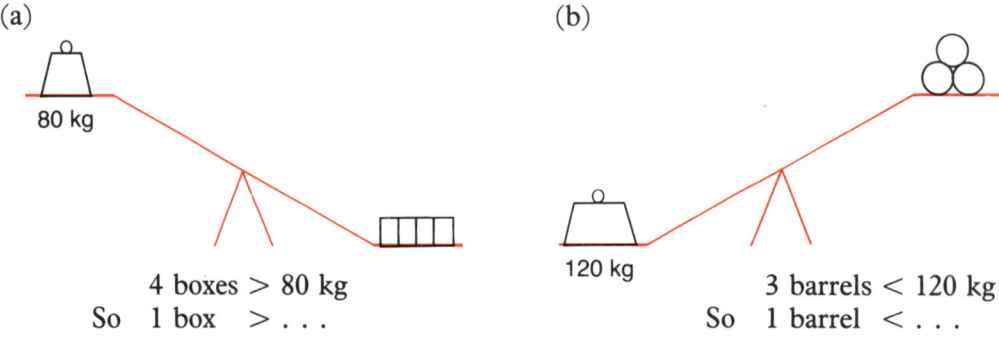

(a) 4 boxes > 80 kg
So   1 box   > . . .

(b) 3 barrels < 120 kg
So   1 barrel < . . .

Once again, we can solve the inequations by using the same method as we used for equations.

Worked examples

(1) Solve $\quad 5x > 40$

Divide both sides by 5. $\quad \dfrac{5x}{5} > \dfrac{40}{5}$

The ×5 and ÷5 cancel out. $\quad x > 8$

(2) Solve $\quad \dfrac{x}{7} < 3$

Multiply both sides by 7. $\quad \dfrac{x}{7} \times 7 < 3 \times 7$

The $\times \tfrac{1}{7}$ and ×7 cancel out. $\quad x < 21$

C2 Solve each of these inequations.

(a) $4x > 28$ (b) $6x < 0$ (c) $\tfrac{1}{2}x < 5$ (d) $\tfrac{1}{4}x > 2$

(e) $2 > \tfrac{1}{8}x$ (f) $48 < 3x$ (g) $20 > 2x$ (h) $8 > 4x$

(i) $36 < \tfrac{2}{3}x$ (j) $\tfrac{1}{16}x < 2$ (k) $\tfrac{1}{5}x < 0.5$ (l) $0.2x < 3$

D Take care with negative numbers!

Consider any true inequation, for example $\quad 1 < 3$.

Multiply both sides by 5. $\qquad\qquad 5 < 15 \quad$ This is true.

Multiply both sides by -2. $\qquad\quad -2 < -6 \quad$ This is false.

Let's investigate this.

D1 Take any true inequation, for example $8 > 2$.

Apply each of the following operations to both sides of it and say whether the new inequation is true or false.

Write your answers like this.

> D1 (a) 8>2   Multiply by 6: 48>12   True

(a) Multiply by 6.   (b) Multiply by $\frac{1}{2}$.   (c) Multiply by -2.
(d) Divide by 2.   (e) Divide by -2.   (f) Multiply by -3.
(g) Divide by 4.   (h) Divide by -4.   (i) Multiply by 7.

D2 Repeat question D1, using another true inequation.

D3 When did you find that the answers were false?

Here is how we could deal with inequations like these:

$$-2x < 40$$

Add $2x$ to both sides. $0 < 40 + 2x$
This is the same as $40 + 2x > 0$ So the $-2x$ is positive now.
Subtract 40 from both sides. $2x > 0 - 40$
                             $2x > -40$
Divide by 2. $x > -20$

$$-24 > -3x$$

Add $3x$ to both sides. $-24 + 3x > 0$ So the $-3x$ is positive now.
Add 24 to both sides. $3x > 0 + 24$
                          $3x > 24$
Divide by 3. $x > 8$

D4 Now solve each of these inequations, remembering that you must make the x term positive each time.

(a) $-3x > 12$ (b) $-2x < -4$ (c) $-x < 5$
(d) $16 < -8x$ (e) $-24 > -2x$ (f) $-x + 7 < 9$

(g) $-2x - 5 > 11$ (h) $1 - 7x < -13$

(i) $5 < -x + 2$ (j) $-3 > 6 - x$

Suppose we want to solve $3 - 2x < 18 + 3x$.

We must get the two x terms together on one side of the inequation and the two numbers together on the other.

$$3 - 2x < 18 + 3x$$

Subtract $3x$ from both sides. $\quad 3 - 2x - 3x < 18$
Subtract 3 from both sides. $\quad\quad -5x < 18 - 3$
$\quad\quad\quad\quad\quad\quad\quad\quad\quad\quad\quad -5x < 15$

Add $5x$ to both sides. $\quad\quad\quad 0 < 15 + 5x$
Subtract 15 from both sides. $\quad -15 < 5x$
$\quad\quad\quad\quad\quad\quad\quad\quad\quad\quad\quad 5x > -15$

Divide by 5. $\quad\quad\quad\quad\quad\quad\quad x > -3$

We can make this simpler by thinking first about the sign of the x term that we shall get if we bring both x terms onto one side of the inequation.

If I subtract $3x$ from both sides, it will appear on the left as $-3x$. With $-2x$ that gives $-5x$. That's a bad move. I'll keep the x terms on the right and they will be positive.

$$3 - 2x < 18 + 3x$$

Add $2x$ to both sides. $\quad\quad\quad\quad\quad 3 < 18 + 3x + 2x$
Subtract 18 from both sides. $\quad 3 - 18 < 5x$
$\quad\quad\quad\quad\quad\quad\quad\quad\quad\quad\quad\quad -15 < 5x$
$\quad\quad\quad\quad\quad\quad\quad\quad\quad\quad\quad\quad 5x > -15$
$\quad\quad\quad\quad\quad\quad\quad\quad\quad\quad\quad\quad x > -3$

D5 Now solve each of these inequations.

Think about the signs of the x terms before you start.

Remember that when you collect them together they should be positive.

(a) $5x + 1 > 2x + 10$ (b) $5 + 7x < 21 - x$

(c) $4 + 3x < 6x - 17$ (d) $3x - 9 < 21 - 7x$

(e) $2 - 8x > 20 - 2x$ (f) $18 + 5x > 8x + 33$

(g) $21x - 12 < 11 - 2x$ (h) $-55 - 11x > 5 + 4x$

(i) $8 - 4x < 5 - 10x$ (j) $4 + 3x > 2 - 5x$

(k) $7 - x < 15 - 3x$ (l) $3x - 2 > 14 + 7x$

E Two other inequality signs

These tins of peas must weigh at least 500 g.

If the tin weighed exactly 500 g, the balance scales would look like this.

If the tin was heavier than 500 g, the balance scales would look like this.

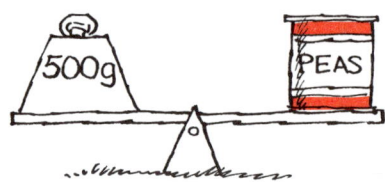

If the weight of a tin of peas is w g, then using symbols we can write

$$w = 500 \qquad\qquad w > 500$$

Putting these together, we have $w \geq 500$.

Mrs Johnston has joined a slimming club.

On her first visit to the club she weighs 75 kg. She must not weigh any more than this when she goes to the club again.

If she stays the same weight, the balance scales will look like this.

If she loses weight, the balance scales will look like this.

If Mrs Johnston's new weight is w kg, we can write

$$w = 75 \qquad\qquad w < 75$$

Putting these together, we have $w \leq 75$.

The symbols $\geq$ (greater than or equal to) and $\leq$ (less than or equal to) can be used in the same way as $>$ and $<$, and the same rules apply to them.

E1 Solve each of these inequations.

(a) $x + 4 \geq 10$ (b) $x - 3 \leq 5$ (c) $3x \geq 15$

(d) $14 \leq 2x$ (e) $5x \geq 13$ (f) $3x - 1 \leq 26$

(g) $4 + 4x \geq 12$ (h) $6 - 2x \leq -2$ (i) $2 - 7x \geq 14 - 4x$

(j) $7x - 11 \geq x + 1$ (k) $3 + 4x \leq -x - 7$ (l) $-5x + 2 \leq 8 - 2x$

Work on inequations often involves brackets. It is usually easiest to deal with this by removing the brackets first and then solving the inequation as before.

Worked example

Dave owns a brewery and cannot decide what size of barrel to use for his beer.

He places the barrels on pallets and stacks the pallets three high on his lorries.

The pallets are 0·1 m high and the floor of the lorry is 1·5 m off the ground.

When the lorry is fully loaded, it must be able to get into the warehouse, which has a door 6 m high.

What must the height of each barrel be?

If each barrel is x m tall, then the height of a pallet and barrel is $(x + 0.1)$ m.

So $3(x + 0.1) + 1.5 < 6$
$3x + 0.3 + 1.5 < 6$
$\qquad 3x < 6 - 0.3 - 1.5$
$\qquad 3x < 4.2$
$\qquad x < 1.4$

Therefore the barrels must be less than 1·4 m tall.

E2 Now solve each of these inequations.

(a) $2(x + 3) > 14$ (b) $3(x - 2) \geqslant 12$ (c) $4(2x + 1) < 6$

(d) $5(x + 0.4) > 2$ (e) $\frac{1}{2}(4x - 6) \leqslant 1$ (f) $\frac{1}{4}(8 - x) \geqslant 5$

(g) $2(x - 2) < x$ (h) $3 + 2(1 + 2x) \geqslant 1$

(i) $4 - (x - 2) < 7$ (j) $1 + 2x \geqslant 3(x - 3)$

(k) $5x - 2 < 2(7 + 3x)$ (l) $9 - 3(x - 1) \geqslant x + 4$

11

Money management 1: pay and income tax

A Pay

Cathy and Colin have just left school. Both of them now have jobs.

Cathy works in the offices of Flash Cash, a company which advises people on money matters. She is paid every month. This is called her **salary**.

Colin works on a building site, where he is paid every week. This is called his **wage**.

Sometimes he is asked to work extra hours, in the evenings or at weekends. This is called **overtime**. He gets paid extra money for every hour's overtime he works.

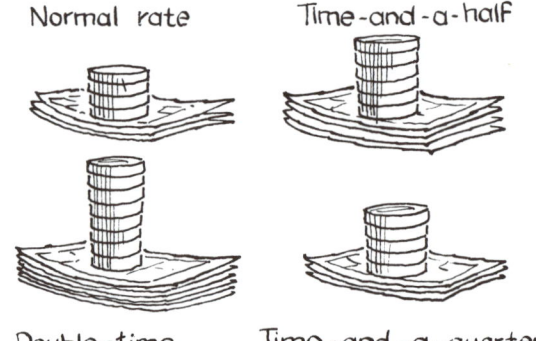

$1\frac{1}{2}$ times the normal rate
  = 'time-and-a-half'.
2 times the normal rate
  = 'double-time'.
$1\frac{1}{4}$ times the normal rate
  = 'time-and-a-quarter'.

Here are some questions about wages and salaries.

A1 Jean works in a shop. She is paid £7500 per year.
Calculate her monthly salary.

A2 Cathy earns £480 per month.
Calculate her annual salary.

A3 Colin works a basic week of 40 hours at £7·80 per hour.
Calculate his total weekly wage.

A4 Bob is paid £156 for a 40-hour week.
Calculate his hourly rate.

A5 John's basic hourly rate is £5·70 for a 40-hour week. He then earns overtime at time-and-a-half.

Last week he worked 46 hours.

Calculate his wage for last week.

A6 (a) Philip usually works a 35-hour week at a basic rate of £3·20 per hour.

He can then be paid overtime at three different rates:
Monday to Friday: Time-and-a-quarter
Saturday: Time-and-a-half
Sunday: Double-time

Last week Philip worked 42 hours, including three hours' overtime during the week, two hours on Saturday and two hours on Sunday.

Calculate his wage for last week.

(b) This week Philip earned £168, including 11 hours' overtime pay for work at the weekend.

Work out how many hours Philip worked at each rate.

B Other types of income

There are other ways that people's earnings can be paid, as well as salaries and wages.

Salespeople are often paid a percentage of the value of the goods they sell, as well as their basic salary. This is called **commission**.

Manufacturing workers are often paid a set amount for every unit of work they complete. This is called **piece-work**.

Here are some questions about commission and piece-work.

B1 Josephine is a sales 'rep' for Gleamyfangs toothpaste. She is paid a basic salary of £3500, plus 16% commission on all her sales.

Last year Josephine sold £44 230 worth of toothpaste.
Calculate her total income last year.

B2 Isabella is a machinist in a knitwear factory. She has no basic wage, but is paid a piece-rate of £2·40 for every dozen jumpers she finishes.

(a) If she finishes 80 dozen jumpers in a week, how much money will she make?
(b) If she finishes a total of 910 jumpers, how much money will she make?
(c) Last week she made £96·80.
How many dozen jumpers did she finish?

C Deductions

The amount of money which people earn is not the same as the amount which they take home, because certain **deductions** are made first. The two main deductions are **national insurance** and **income tax**.

National insurance is a percentage of a person's income that is deducted by the government to pay for things like sick pay, social security, etc.

Income tax is also deducted from a person's earnings by the government. The money raised is used to pay for items like defence, roads, etc.

People do not pay income tax on the whole of their income: they are allowed to earn a certain amount which is not taxed. This **allowance** is greater for a married man than for a single person. The amount of income on which tax is paid is called **taxable income**. In 1988 the basic rate of income tax was 25%.

A person's earnings before the deductions are made are called their **gross income**.

A person's earnings after the deductions are made are called their **net income**.

Worked example

James is a nurse. He has an annual gross income of £7910. He pays 7% national insurance and 25% income tax.

He has a single person's tax allowance of £2425.

Calculate his annual net income.

National insurance = 7% of £7910
                  = £553·70

Total allowances = £2425

Taxable income   = £7910 − £2425
                  = £5485

Income tax   = 25% of £5485
                  = £1371·25

Total deductions = £553·70 + £1371·25
                  = £1924·95

Net income   = £7910 − £1924·95
                  = £5985·05

Use the following table of allowances, and a tax rate of 25%, in the questions which follow.

Allowance	Amount
Single person's	£2425
Married man's	£3795
Wife's earned income	£2425
Single person's (aged 65–79)	£2960
Single person's (aged 80+)	£3070
Married man's (aged 65–79)	£4675
Married man's (aged 80+)	£4845

C1 George is a storekeeper in a factory. He earns £132 per week before deductions are made. He pays 7% national insurance. He is married.

(a) Calculate his annual wage.

(b) Calculate how much income tax George must pay each week.

C2 Over the year, Trudi, who is unmarried, paid £2153·25 in income tax.

(a) What was Trudi's gross income for the year?

(b) If she also paid £3 per month to her trade union and 7% national insurance, what was Trudi's net monthly income?

C3 From this group of part-time workers,

(a) Who pays no income tax?

(b) How much tax must each of the other workers pay?

(c) Fred is offered the chance to work one more day every week. Should he take this opportunity?

Give a reason for your answer.

(d) Why do you think Sandy refused his rise this year?
Do you think he made the right decision?

Give a reason for your answer.

D Higher tax rates

People who earn a lot of money pay a higher rate of tax on some of their income. In 1988 they paid 40% on the part of their taxable income which was greater than £19 500.

We can draw a 'tax tub' to show this:

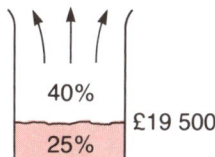

Here is an example to show how this higher tax band would be used.

Vicki is a concert pianist. She earned £32 000 in 1988.

Work out how much income tax she had to pay.

Taxable income = £32 000 − £2425
= £29 575

Imagine Vicki's taxable income poured into a 'tax tub':

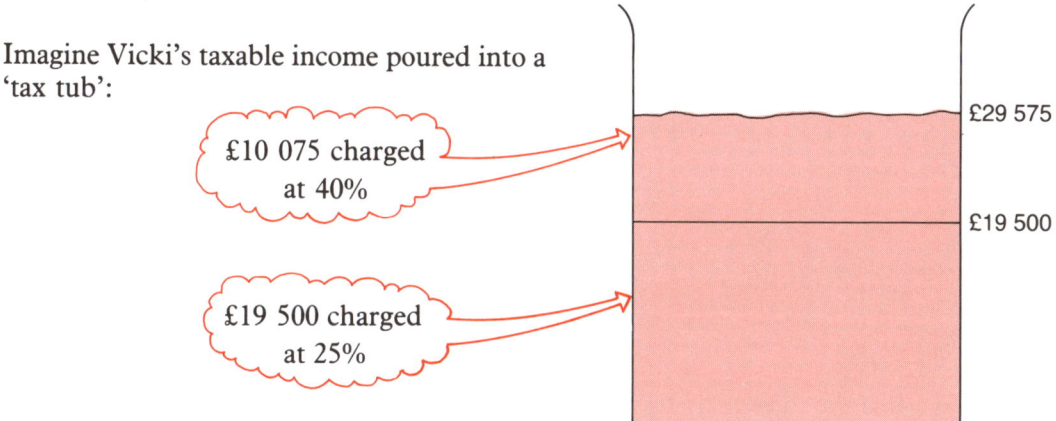

£10 075 charged at 40%

£19 500 charged at 25%

25% of £19 500 = £4875
40% of £10 075 = £4030
Total tax = £8905

D1 Calculate the tax which should be paid by each of these people.

(a) Rantin' Robin is a famous pop star. In 1988 he earned £635 072 from his first tour of Ayrshire.

(b) Sam Sly sells fridges in Alaska, sand in Saudi Arabia and broken boomerangs in Tasmania. His wife says his explosives business is also booming. He earned £27 450.

We can also work out income tax using a flow chart like this.

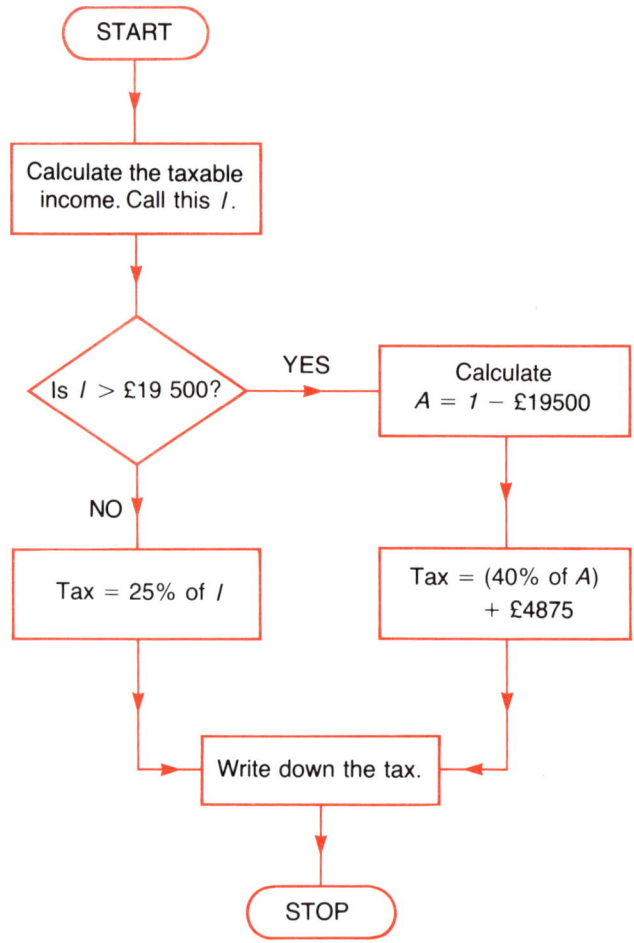

D2 Use the flow chart to work out the income tax payable on each of these taxable incomes.

(a) £42 000   (b) £37 075   (c) £23 947   (d) £2 556 721

Now tax your brain with this final example:

D3 Sue earned £67 500 in 1988. She is single and pays 7% national insurance.

Louis earned £49 500 in 1988. He is married and pays 7% national insurance.

Who had the higher net monthly income, and by how much?

2 Square roots

A Calculations with square roots

Suppose we want to calculate the length of AD.

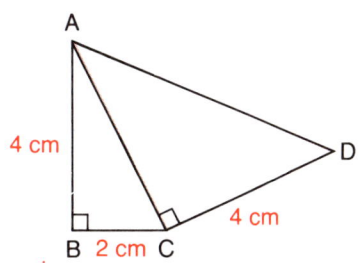

We can work out the length like this.

1 Before calculating AD, we have to calculate the length of AC, using Pythagoras' rule.

$$AC^2 = AB^2 + BC^2$$
$$= 4^2 + 2^2$$
$$= 16 + 4$$
$$= 20$$
$$AC = \sqrt{20} \text{ cm}$$

2 There are two ways in which we can continue.

Method A

Use a calculator to get an **approximate** value for $\sqrt{20}$.

$$AC = \sqrt{20} \approx 4 \cdot 47 \quad \text{(to 2 d.p.)}$$
$$AD^2 = AC^2 + CD^2$$
$$= 4 \cdot 47^2 + 4^2$$
$$= 19 \cdot 98 + 16$$
$$= 35 \cdot 98$$
$$AD \approx 5 \cdot 998 \text{ cm}$$

Another approximation

A third approximation

Method B

Use $\sqrt{20}$ in its exact form.

$$AC = \sqrt{20}$$
$$AD^2 = AC^2 + CD^2$$
$$= (\sqrt{20})^2 + 4^2$$
$$= 20 + 16$$
$$= 36$$
$$AD = 6 \text{ cm}$$

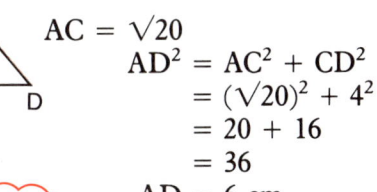

Method B is the more accurate, since no approximations are used.

When we have to use the result of a calculation involving square roots to work out something else, it is important to leave the square roots in the form $\sqrt{\ldots}$ rather than use an approximation.

Here are some examples for you to try.

Remember: Leave the square roots in their exact form.

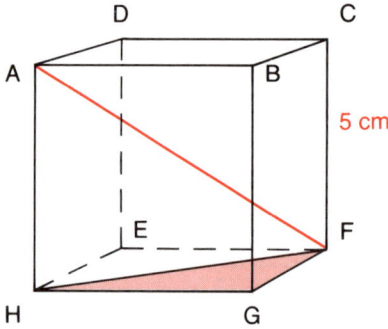

A1 ABCDEFGH is a cube of side 5 cm.

(a) Calculate the length of FH, using triangle FGH.

(b) Use the result of this calculation to work out the length of AF.

A2 Calculate the length of the space diagonal marked in this diagram.

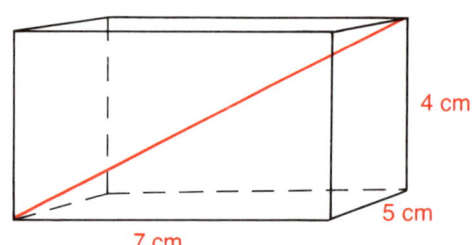

B Surds

Square roots like $\sqrt{200}$ and $\sqrt{5}$, which do not have an exact value, are called **surds**.

Square roots like $\sqrt{4}$ and $\sqrt{25}$ are not surds, since they can be replaced by exact values (2 and 5, respectively).

B1 Which of the following square roots
(a) are surds (b) are not surds

$\sqrt{3}$ $\sqrt{36}$ $\sqrt{49}$ $\sqrt{6}$ $\sqrt{900}$ $\sqrt{90}$ $\sqrt{169}$ $\sqrt{203}$ $\sqrt{2}$ $\sqrt{9}$

The rest of this chapter deals with surds.

C Equivalent surds: products and factors

C1 (a) Use Pythagoras' rule to calculate the length of AC. Leave your answer as a square root.

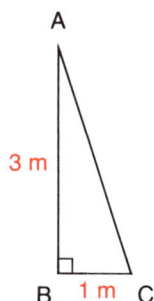

(b) Here is a $\times \sqrt{2}$ enlargement of triangle ABC.

(i) Calculate the length of A'C'.

(ii) Copy and complete the following working.

$$A'C' = \sqrt{2}\,(AC)$$
$$\sqrt{\ldots} = \sqrt{2}\,\sqrt{\ldots}$$

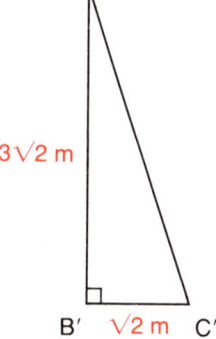

(c) Here is a $\times 2$ enlargement of triangle ABC.

(i) Calculate the length of A"C".

(ii) Copy and complete the following working.

$$A''C'' = 2(\ldots)$$
$$\ldots = 2\ldots$$

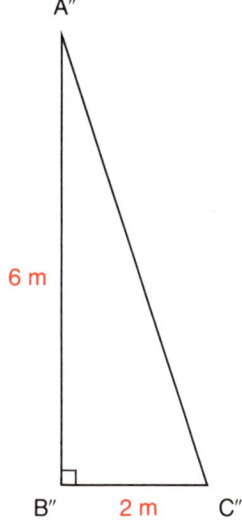

Look at your answer to question C1(b).

You should have found that

$\sqrt{20} = \sqrt{2}\,\sqrt{10}$.

We can re-write this as a general rule, which works every time.

Product rule: $\sqrt{a}\,\sqrt{b} = \sqrt{ab}$

C2 Simplify each of the following surds, using the product rule.

(a) $\sqrt{6}\ \sqrt{2}$ (b) $\sqrt{7}\ \sqrt{3}$ (c) $\sqrt{3}\ \sqrt{6}$ (d) $\sqrt{5}\ \sqrt{6}$

(e) $\sqrt{10}\ \sqrt{3}$ (f) $\sqrt{17}\ \sqrt{5}$ (g) $\sqrt{18}\ \sqrt{10}$ (h) $\sqrt{18}\ \sqrt{2}$

(i) $\sqrt{20}\ \sqrt{5}$ (j) $\sqrt{20}\ \sqrt{45}$ (k) $\sqrt{37}\ \sqrt{13}$ (l) $\sqrt{72}\ \sqrt{30}$

Look at your answer to question C1(c).

You should have found that $\sqrt{40} = 2\sqrt{10}$.

Using the product rule the other way round, we get   *(This is a perfect square.)*

$$\sqrt{40} = \sqrt{4}\ \sqrt{10}$$
$$= 2\ \sqrt{10}$$

We can do this where we have

$\sqrt{(\text{perfect square} \times \text{another number})}$

We will call this rule the 'factor rule'.   *(a is a perfect square.)*

Factor rule: $\sqrt{ab} = \sqrt{a}\ \sqrt{b}$
$= A\ \sqrt{b}$ $A = \sqrt{a}$

C3 Simplify each of the following surds, using the factor rule.

The first one has been done for you.

(a) $\sqrt{75} = \sqrt{25}\ \sqrt{3} = 5\sqrt{3}$

(b) $\sqrt{72}$ (c) $\sqrt{500}$ (d) $\sqrt{360}$ (e) $\sqrt{245}$

(f) $\sqrt{512}$ (g) $\sqrt{432}$ (h) $\sqrt{384}$ (i) $\sqrt{972}$

(Same number after the square root sign.)

Expressions like $5\sqrt{3}$ and $2\sqrt{3}$ are called **like** surds.

Expressions like $3\sqrt{5}$ and $2\sqrt{7}$ are called **unlike** surds.

As with other expressions involving like terms (e.g. $2a + 3a$), we can combine like surds together. Here is an example.

$2\sqrt{3} + 5\sqrt{2} - 3\sqrt{2} + \sqrt{3}$
$= 2\sqrt{3} + \sqrt{3} + 5\sqrt{2} - 3\sqrt{2}$
$= 3\sqrt{3} + 2\sqrt{2}$

*(This is like
$2a + 5b - 3b + a$
$= 2a + a + 5b - 3b$
$= 3a + 2b$)*

C4 Simplify each of the following expressions by collecting together the like surds.

(a) $2\sqrt{7} + 3\sqrt{3} - \sqrt{7}$ (b) $8\sqrt{5} - 3\sqrt{3} + 4\sqrt{3}$

(c) $7\sqrt{11} + 2\sqrt{3} - 5\sqrt{3} - 6\sqrt{11}$ (d) $6\sqrt{5} - 3\sqrt{2} - 9\sqrt{5}$

(e) $10\sqrt{50} - 6\sqrt{2} + 2\sqrt{5}$ (f) $3\sqrt{8} + 2\sqrt{32} - 6\sqrt{6} + 2\sqrt{12}$

(Use the factor rule.)

D Equivalent surds: fractions

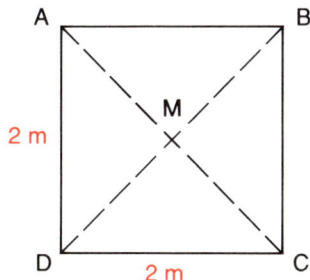

ABCD is a square of side 2 m and M is the midpoint of AC and BD.

We are going to work out the length of MC in two different ways.

First method

D1 (a) Use Pythagoras' rule to work out the length of AC.

(b) Hence calculate the length of MC.

Second method

Triangle CMD is a reduction of triangle ADC.

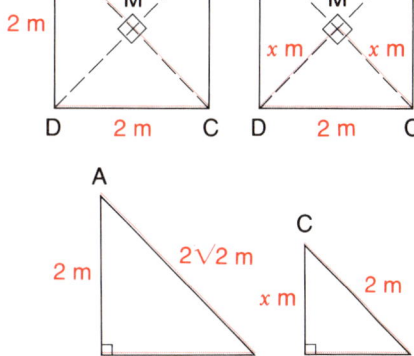

When we draw these two triangles facing in the same direction, we see that the scale factor of the reduction is given by

$$\frac{CD}{AC} = \frac{2}{2\sqrt{2}} = \frac{1}{\sqrt{2}}$$

D2 Use this information to work out MC.

D3 Copy and complete the following statements.

MC = ... m (from question D1)

MC = ... m (from question D2)

D4 We now have two ways of writing the same number (even though they do not look the same). Check that they are equal, by squaring them both.

D5 Show that the surds in each of the following lists are equal, by squaring them.

(a) $\sqrt{\frac{3}{4}}, \frac{\sqrt{3}}{2}, \frac{3}{2\sqrt{3}}$ (b) $\frac{1}{\sqrt{5}}, \sqrt{\frac{25}{125}}, \frac{\sqrt{5}}{5}$

(c) $\sqrt{\frac{2}{3}}, \frac{2\sqrt{2}}{\sqrt{12}}, \frac{\sqrt{6}}{3}$

Here is another way of showing that $\frac{1}{\sqrt{2}}$ and $\frac{\sqrt{2}}{2}$ are equal.

$$\frac{1}{\sqrt{2}} = \frac{1}{\sqrt{2}} \times \frac{\sqrt{2}}{\sqrt{2}} = \frac{\sqrt{2}}{\sqrt{2}\sqrt{2}} = \frac{\sqrt{2}}{\sqrt{4}} = \frac{\sqrt{2}}{2}$$

These numbers are the same.

This fraction is equal to 1. Multiplying a number by 1 does not change its value.

This method is very useful as it gets rid of the surd on the bottom line.

Here is another example.

$$\frac{2}{\sqrt{5}} = \frac{2}{\sqrt{5}} \times \frac{\sqrt{5}}{\sqrt{5}} = \frac{2\sqrt{5}}{\sqrt{5}\sqrt{5}} = \frac{2\sqrt{5}}{\sqrt{25}} = \frac{2\sqrt{5}}{5}$$

D6 Simplify each of the following surds.

(a) $\frac{1}{\sqrt{3}}$ (b) $\frac{3}{\sqrt{6}}$ (c) $\frac{7}{\sqrt{7}}$ (d) $\frac{2}{\sqrt{6}}$ (e) $\frac{1}{\sqrt{15}}$

(f) $\frac{1}{\sqrt{50}}$ (g) $\frac{6}{\sqrt{12}}$ (h) $\frac{8}{\sqrt{17}}$ (i) $\frac{10}{\sqrt{1000}}$ (j) $\frac{32}{\sqrt{80}}$

E Miscellany

Use all the methods you have learnt to simplify the following expressions.

E1 $\sqrt{175}$ **E2** $\sqrt{7}\sqrt{2}$ **E3** $\sqrt{2} + \sqrt{8}$

E4 $\sqrt{40} + \sqrt{8}\sqrt{5}$ **E5** $\frac{\sqrt{27}}{3}$ **E6** $\sqrt{75} - 2\sqrt{5}$

E7 $4\sqrt{3} \times 2\sqrt{12}$ **E8** $\sqrt{\frac{4}{9} - \frac{1}{3}}$ **E9** $3\sqrt{5} \div \sqrt{45}$

E10 $\frac{7}{\sqrt{10}}$ **E11** $\frac{4}{\sqrt{2}} + \frac{3}{2}$ **E12** $\frac{17}{\sqrt{3}} - \frac{5}{3}$

E13 $\frac{6}{7} - \sqrt{\frac{1}{7}}$ **E14** $\frac{4\sqrt{3} + \sqrt{18}}{\sqrt{27}}$ **E15** $2\sqrt{2}\left(\sqrt{5} + \frac{3}{\sqrt{2}}\right)$

E16 $4\sqrt{3}\left(\sqrt{12} + \frac{1}{\sqrt{2}}\right)$

F Evaluating square roots

There are two methods of working out square roots (without using the $\sqrt{}$ button on your calculator!).

Method 1

We know that $\sqrt{25} = 5$ because $5 \times 5 = 25$, or $25 \div 5 = 5$.

We can write      These numbers are the same.

If we try to calculate $\sqrt{6}$ in this way it is not so easy, but the same idea can be used.

1   6 lies between 4 and 9,

so $\sqrt{6}$ lies between 2 and 3.

Number	(Number)²
0	0
1	1
2	4
	6
3	9

2   Try $\sqrt{6} = 2\cdot 4$.

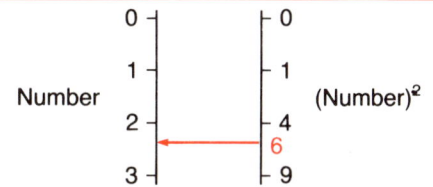

We want these numbers to be the same.

They are not the same, so we must try again.

3   Use the average of the two numbers printed in red as the next try.

$$\frac{2\cdot 4 + 2\cdot 5}{2} = 2\cdot 45$$

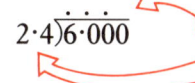

They are not the same, so we must carry out step 3 again.

$$\frac{2\cdot 45 + 2\cdot 449}{2} = 2\cdot 4495$$

$2\cdot 4495\overline{)6\cdot 000\,00}$ gives $2\cdot 449\,48$

They are still not the same, but each time we are getting closer.

We can repeat step 3 again and again until we reach the required degree of accuracy. For example, if we are working to two decimal places, we can write

$\sqrt{6} = 2{\cdot}45$ (to 2 d.p.)

This method is called an **iterative process** because it repeats itself again and again (iterates).

F1 Calculate the following square roots to three decimal places using the iterative process shown above.

The first one has been started for you.

(a) $\sqrt{13}$
13 lies between 9 and 16,
so $\sqrt{13}$ lies between 3 and 4.
Try 3·6.

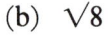

(b) $\sqrt{8}$ (c) $\sqrt{29}$ (d) $\sqrt{79}$

(e) $\sqrt{140}$ (f) $\sqrt{218}$

Method 2: the rote method

This method was taught in schools before calculators were in general use. The pupils were not expected to understand the process, only how to use it. Therefore it was called the **rote method**.

Here is how a textbook published in 1948 explained it.

Find the square root of 207 936.

```
              4  5  6
          4 ) 20'79'36
              16
           85  479
               425
          906  5436
               5436
```
∴ $\sqrt{207936} = 456$

(1) Mark off the digits in groups of two, beginning from the right.
(2) Find the greatest number whose square is less than 20.
(3) Place 4 in the answer, and subtract the square of 4 from 20. Bring down the next group.
(4) Double the answer (4) and using 8? as a trial divisor, obtain 5 as the next figure in the answer. Place the same figure 5 after the 8, multiply 85 by 5 and subtract. Bring down the next group.
(5) Double the answer (45) and using 90? as a trial divisor proceed as before.

We shall now use this method to work out $\sqrt{1369}$.

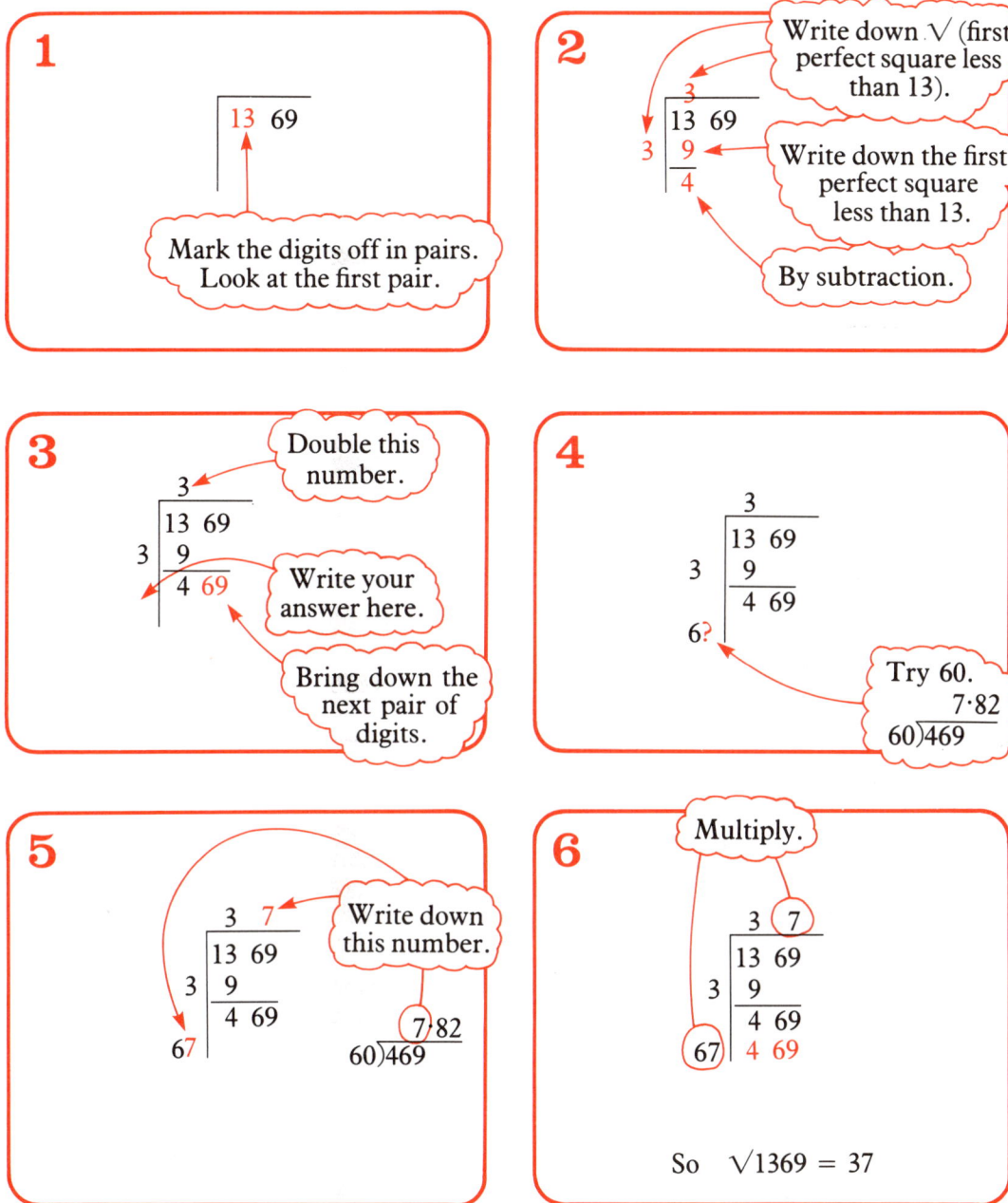

F2 Use the rote method to calculate each of the following square roots.

(a) $\sqrt{1764}$ (b) $\sqrt{7225}$ (c) $\sqrt{101\,761}$ (d) $\sqrt{552\,049}$

F3 Now try $\sqrt{343\,396}$. What happens?

Can you find a way to overcome this?

Money management 2: index numbers

A Calculating index numbers

FT Index Falls

RETAIL PRICE INDEX SOARS

Share Index Peaks

Dow-Jones Index Rockets

You may have seen headlines like these in newspapers, and wondered what the word 'index' meant. Usually, an index is a list of the contents of a book and where to find them. Obviously, 'index' does not have this meaning here!

Perhaps the people at Flash Cash can shed some light on the subject.

Index? That's easy! It's a list showing how the price of an object increases or decreases over a number of years. It's all done by percentages.

Let's look at this in a bit more detail.

The year in which the index starts is called the **base year**. The price of the object in that year is given the index number 100 (since its price then is 100% of its base-year price).

If the same object cost 20% more a year later, its index number then would be 120.

If the same object had cost 15% less the year before, its index number then would have been 85.

Worked example

Compile an index for these prices of Saturn bars between 1985 and 1988, taking 1986 as the base year.

Year	1985	1986	1987	1988
Price	10p	12p	13p	14p

1 Give the base year the index number 100.

   1986: 12p   100

2 Work out the percentage increases or decreases in relation to the base year.

1985: 2p decrease   1987: 1p increase   1988: 3p increase
$\frac{2}{12} \times 100 = 16{\cdot}67\%$ $\frac{1}{12} \times 100 = 8{\cdot}33\%$ $\frac{3}{12} \times 100 = 25\%$

3 Work out the index numbers.

1986		100
1985	100 − 16·67 = 83·33	83
1987	100 + 8·33 = 108·33	108
1988	100 + 25 = 125	125

Round off to the nearest whole number.

Compile index numbers for the following lists of sweet prices, using the same method.

A1 Chewies: base year 1985.

Year	1983	1984	1985	1986	1987
Price	9p	9p	10p	12p	13p

A2 Nebula bars: base year 1988.

Year	1984	1985	1986	1987	1988
Price	25p	27p	30p	32p	35p

A3 Goody Bags: base year 1987.

Year	1985	1986	1987	1988	1989
Price	60p	64p	68p	70p	75p

B Calculating prices

Here are some lists of index numbers for some sweet prices.
For each list, work out the price of the sweet in each year.

The first one has been started for you.

B1 Jolly Lollies: base-year price 50p.

Year	1985	1986	1987	1988
Index	98	100	103	112

B1 1986 (base year): Price = 50p

1985: Decrease of 2%   1987: Increase
2% of 50p = 1p   3% of
Price = 49p   Price =

1988: Increase of 12%
12% of 50p =

B2 Beatel Juice: base-year price £1·50.

Year	1998	1999	2000	2001	2002
Index	100	110	116	124	136

B3 Mega Chocs: base-year price £3·75.

Year	1987	1988	1989	1990
Index	85	92	97	100

C Using index numbers

C1 The index numbers for the prices of certain sports goods are as follows:

Year	1989	1990	1991	1992	1993
Index	98	100	101	103	106

Which of these goods had a price rise below that of the index?

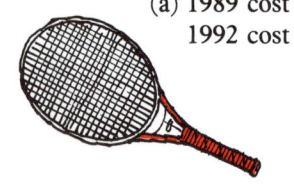
(a) 1989 cost £45.60
    1992 cost £48.80

(b) 1991 cost £15.99
    1992 cost £16.15

(c) 1990 cost £37.75
    1993 cost £40

C2 The employees of I. Boss plc agree that their wages will rise in line with the Average Wages Index.

Year	1987	1988	1989	1990	1991	1992
Average Wages Index	82	100	109	123	123	148

(a) If Joe's annual wage in 1987 was £10 562, what wage should he expect in 1989?

(b) During which period was there a wages freeze?

(c) In 1988, Barbara's annual salary was £12 750. By which year had her salary increased to £18 870?

C3 The populations (in millions) of the United Kingdom and the USA are recorded over a period of time, and projections are made for future years.

Year	1975	1980	1985	1990	1995	2000
UK	56·4	57·5	58·7	60·0	61·4	62·8
USA	213·9	224·1	235·7	246·6	256·0	264·4

(a) Calculate index numbers for the populations, using 1990 as the base year.

(b) Draw a graph for each country to show the change in the index number over this period. (Use the same axes for both graphs.)

(c) Describe how the populations of the UK and the USA have grown during this period.

3 Special angles

A Exact values of trigonometric ratios

A1 ABCD is a square of side 1 cm.

(a) Use Pythagoras' rule to calculate the length of the diagonal BD, leaving your answer as a square root.

(b) Draw out triangle BCD separately, and mark all its sides and angles.

(c) From triangle BCD, write down the values of sin 45°, cos 45° and tan 45°, leaving your answers as square roots if necessary.

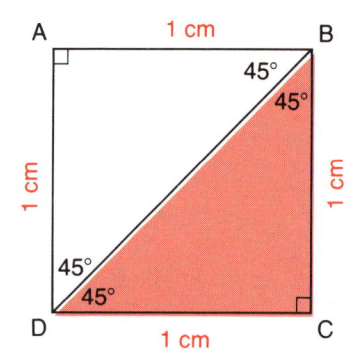

A2 ABC is an equilateral triangle with side 2 cm.

(a) Use Pythagoras' rule to calculate the length of the altitude AD, leaving your answer as a square root.

(b) Draw out triangle ACD separately, and mark all its sides and angles.

(c) From triangle ACD, write down the values of sin 30°, cos 30°, tan 30°, sin 60°, cos 60° and tan 60°, leaving your answers as square roots if necessary.

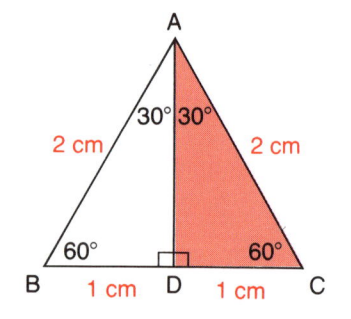

A3 Copy and complete this table, using your answers to questions A1 and A2.

	30°	45°	60°
sine			
cosine			
tangent			

These are called the **exact values** of the trigonometric ratios for these angles.

A4 Why do you think they are called 'exact values'?

B Properties of angles: an investigation

B1 Write down the values of

(a) sin 30° (b) $\sin^2 30°$ (c) cos 30°
(d) $\cos^2 30°$ (e) $\sin^2 30° + \cos^2 30°$

Leave your answers as surds if necessary.

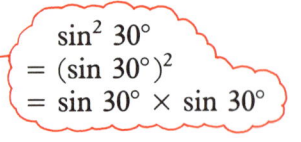

$\sin^2 30°$
$= (\sin 30°)^2$
$= \sin 30° \times \sin 30°$

B2 Repeat question B1 for 45° and 60°.

B3 In general, what can you say about $\sin^2 x° + \cos^2 x°$?

B4 (a) Write down the values of sin 30°, cos 30° and tan 30°.

(b) Can you find a relationship between sin 30°, cos 30° and tan 30°?

(c) Check whether your idea works with 45° and 60°.

B5 (a) Write down the values of the sines and cosines of pairs of angles that add up to 90°, e.g. sin 30° and cos 60°.

(b) Can you find a relationship between them?

(c) Write it down as a general rule.

B6 Try out your rules for a number of other angles. Use a scientific calculator to help you, if you have one.

C Using exact values

C1 Mrs Brown's cat Plato is stuck up a tree.
Her son James rushes to its rescue.

When he is 20 m away from the tree, he sees the cat at an angle of elevation of 45°.

Calculate the height of the cat above the ground.

C2 Calculate the exact value of the unknown marked **?** in each of these triangles.

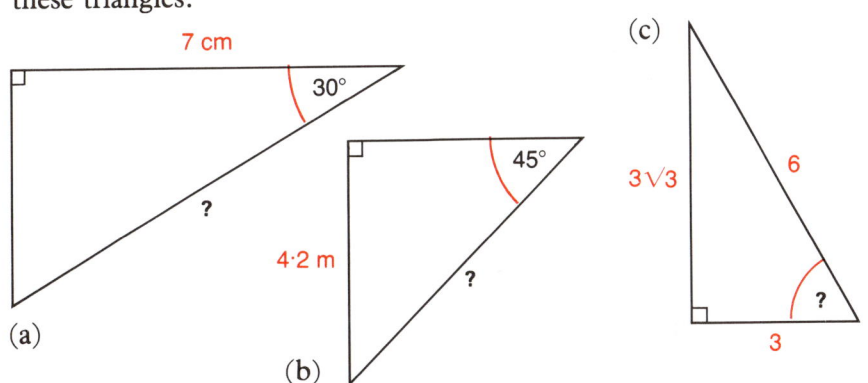

C3 Here are a map showing three checkpoints on an orienteering course and the instructions for getting from one of them to another.

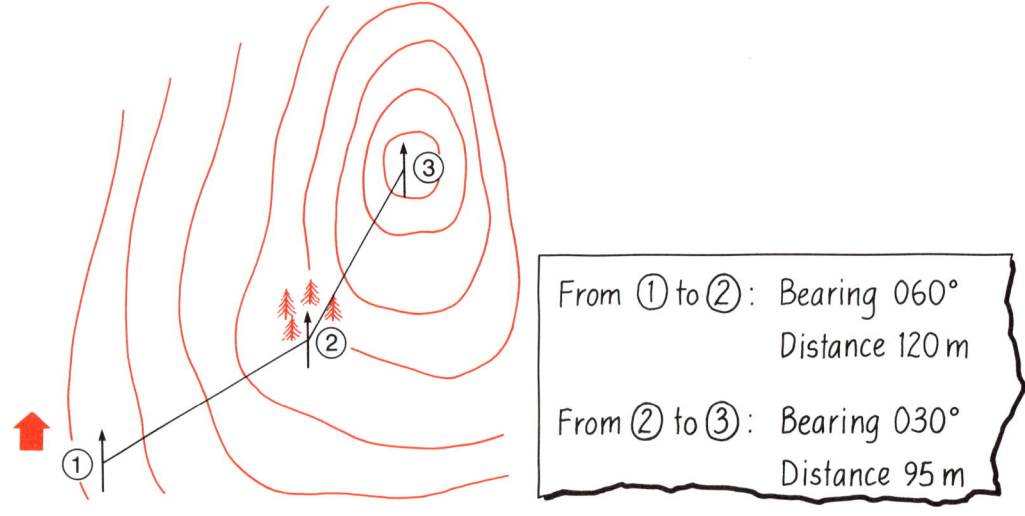

From ① to ②: Bearing 060°
Distance 120 m

From ② to ③: Bearing 030°
Distance 95 m

Calculate how far (a) north, (b) east of checkpoint 1 you would find checkpoint 3.

C4 Neil is cutting two set-squares from this rectangular piece of wood.

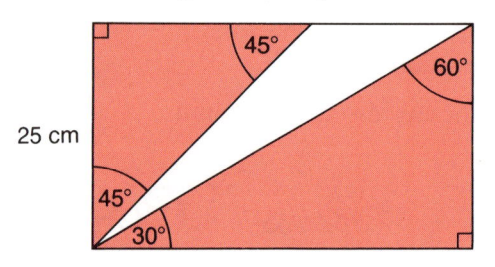

(a) Calculate the exact lengths of the sides of each set-square.

(b) Work out exactly how much wood is wasted.

C5 Margaret is standing on top of Ben Tarsuinn, which is 500 m higher than the surrounding countryside.

She sees a hut on a bearing of 090° and at an angle of depression of 30°, and a tent on a bearing of 180° and at an angle of depression of 45°.

(a) Draw a sketch to show this information.

(b) Calculate the exact distance from the hut to the tent.

Consolidation 1

Inequations

1 Solve each of the following inequations.

(a) $3x > 24$
(b) $\frac{x}{2} \leq 13$
(c) $x + 4 \geq -9$
(d) $3x - 9 < 21$
(e) $4x \leq 2x - 4$
(f) $5x + 12 > 8 + 3x$
(g) $3x + 4 \geq 14 - 2x$
(h) $\frac{1}{4}x - 7 > 3$
(i) $\frac{2}{3}x + 4 \leq 6$
(j) $-2x > 12$
(k) $-5x + 8 \geq 23$
(l) $3x - 7 > 5 + 6x$
(m) $2x - 1 \cdot 5 \leq 5x$
(n) $7 - 3x < 2x + 12$
(o) $3(x + 2) \geq 0$
(p) $4(5 - x) \leq 4$
(q) $1 + 2(2x + 3) \geq 8$
(r) $4(2 - x) < 5(1 - 2x)$
(s) $\frac{1}{2}(x + 4) > 8$
(t) $\frac{1}{3}(2x - 3) \leq x$

2 The jib of this crane can be raised or lowered about a point 1·9 m above the ground. Form an inequation from this information if the crane has to be able to go under the bridge. From this, deduce what values x can take.

Since this distance can vary, we shall call it x m.

7·2m

1·9 m

Pay and income tax

Use the allowances shown on page 15 and a tax rate of 25%.

1 Richard works in an office and receives a salary of £685 per month. What are his gross earnings in a year?

2 Elaine works on a building site and receives a wage of £11·50 per hour. Her basic week is 37 hours.

Last week she worked 39 hours, with the overtime paid at time-and-a-half.

What was Elaine's gross pay last week?

3 If Richard in question 1 is married and pays 7% of his pay in national insurance, how much income tax does he pay each month?

4 Aileen is the sales manager for a small publishing company. She earns a basic annual salary of £10 500 plus 7% commission on sales.

Owing to the publication of a new maths book, last year's sales rocketed to £360 000.

(a) Calculate Aileen's gross annual salary for last year.

(b) If she paid 7% in national insurance, calculate how much Aileen paid in income tax last year.

(c) Calculate her net annual salary.

5 Ian gets paid a piece-rate of £4·75 for every complete dozen pairs of jeans he finishes.

(a) If he finished 576 pairs this week, calculate his gross wage.

(b) Last week he finished 475 pairs. Calculate his gross wage for last week.

(c) Two weeks ago, his gross wage was £213·75. Write down the maximum and minimum numbers of pairs of jeans he could have finished.

(d) If Ian is single and pays 7% national insurance, work out his net weekly wage for each of the last three weeks.

Square roots

1 ABCDE is a square-based pyramid with base length 12 cm and slant height 20 cm.

Calculate the exact vertical height of the pyramid.

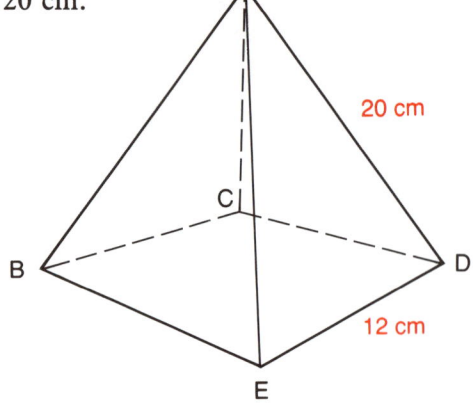

2 Simplify each of the following expressions.

(a) $\sqrt{6}\sqrt{2}$ (b) $\sqrt{500}$ (c) $5\sqrt{3} + 6\sqrt{27}$
(d) $2\sqrt{2} + 3\sqrt{50}$ (e) $\sqrt{27}\sqrt{3}$ (f) $\sqrt{368}$

3 Re-write each of the following expressions with no surds on the bottom line.

(a) $\dfrac{5}{\sqrt{6}}$ (b) $\dfrac{2\sqrt{3}}{\sqrt{2}}$ (c) $\dfrac{7}{2\sqrt{5}}$ (d) $\dfrac{9}{3\sqrt{3}}$ (e) $\dfrac{5\sqrt{13}}{2\sqrt{52}}$

4 Use an iterative process to calculate each of the following square roots to three decimal places.

(a) $\sqrt{12}$ (b) $\sqrt{33}$ (c) $\sqrt{24}$

Index numbers

1 This table shows two indexes which have 1999 as the base year.

Year	1998	1999	2000	2001	2002	2003	2004
Microscoff index	98	100	105	109	117	119	123
Worktoken index	96	100	106	110	112	115	120

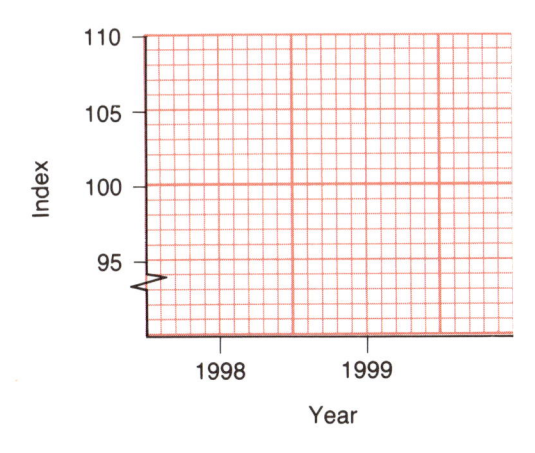

(a) Draw a graph of these indexes, plotting both of them on the same axes.

Use your graph and the table to answer the questions below.

(b) In which year was the Worktoken index higher than the Microscoff index?

(c) Find the percentage increase in the price of Microscoff by the year 2002, compared with its price in the base year.

(d) In 1999 the average Worktoken (wage) was 250 megapounds. Calculate the average Worktoken in 2004.

(e) During which period was the price of Microscoff increasing most rapidly?

2 Here are the prices of a packet of crisps over four years.

Year	1998	1999	2000	2001
Price	50p	53p	58p	65p

Compile index numbers for these prices, taking 1999 as the base year.

Special angles

1 Calculate the exact length of the side of this square.

(square with diagonal $5\sqrt{2}$ cm)

2 Calculate the exact length of the side of this equilateral triangle, and its area.

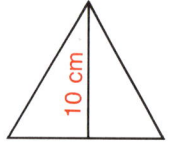

(equilateral triangle with height 10 cm)

3 Arrange the following in order of size, from smallest to largest:

   sin 60°   cos 60°   tan 45°   cos 45°

4 John sees an eagle at an angle of elevation of 45°. He estimates its distance from him to be 50 m.

Calculate the height of the eagle, leaving your answer as a square root if necessary.

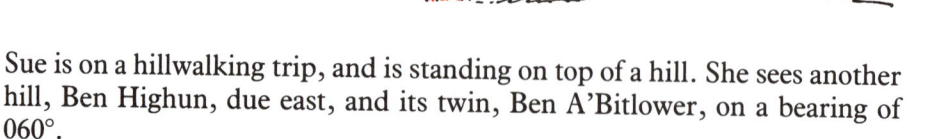

5 Sue is on a hillwalking trip, and is standing on top of a hill. She sees another hill, Ben Highun, due east, and its twin, Ben A'Bitlower, on a bearing of 060°.

Hugh is standing 6 km away, on the top of Ben Highun and sees Ben A'Bitlower due north of him.

Exactly how far apart are Ben Highun and Ben A'Bitlower?

4 Graphs (1)

A Number machines

Do you remember number machines like this?

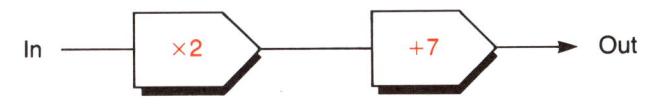

In ──[×2]──[+7]──▶ Out

If you feed in the number 4, the number 15 comes out:

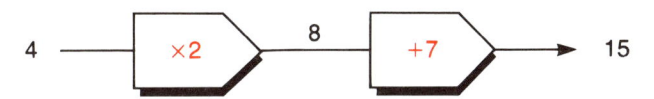

4 ──[×2]──8──[+7]──▶ 15

A1 Here is a chain of machines.

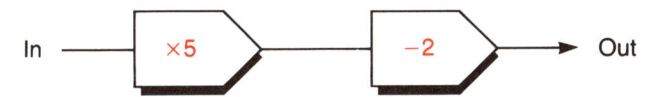

In ──[×5]──[−2]──▶ Out

What comes out if you feed in
(a) 6 (b) 4 (c) −2

A2 Here is another chain of machines.

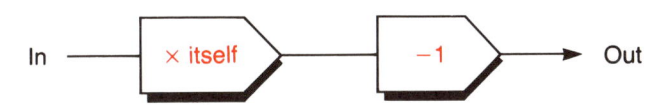

In ──[× itself]──[−1]──▶ Out

If you feed in 6, 35 comes out:

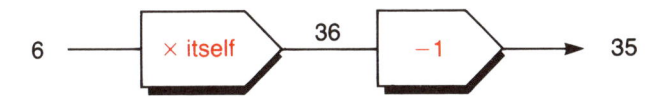

6 ──[× itself]──36──[−1]──▶ 35

What comes out if you feed in (a) 2 (b) 12 (c) −1

A3 Here is another chain of machines.

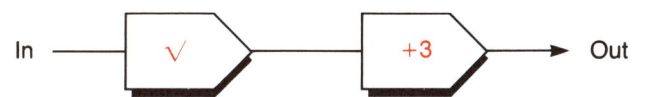

In ──[√]──[+3]──▶ Out

If you feed in 9, either 6 comes out or 0 comes out.

(a) Can you explain why this happens?
(b) What comes out if you feed in
(i) 25 (ii) 0 (iii) 49

A4 Look at this chain of machines.

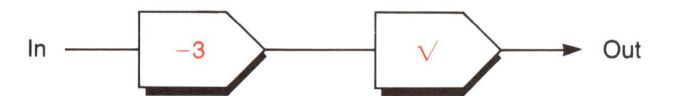

In ⟶ −3 ⟶ √ ⟶ Out

(a) What happens when you feed in (i) 28   (ii) 9·25   (iii) 9

(b) Explain what happens when you feed in 0.

Some chains of number machines are special. They are called **functions**.

For a machine chain to be a function, two things must be true:

(1) All numbers can go in.
(2) Only one number comes out for each number that goes in.

Here are two number machines.

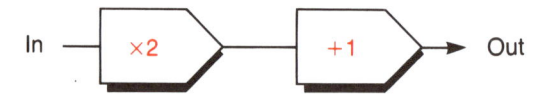

In ⟶ ×2 ⟶ +1 ⟶ Out

This is a function.

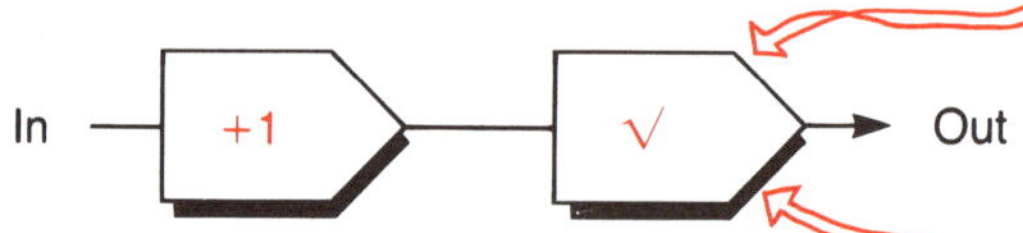

In ⟶ +1 ⟶ √ ⟶ Out

This is not a function.

> Square roots have two values.
>
> We can't find square roots of negative numbers, so numbers smaller than −1 cannot go in.

A5 Which of these chains are functions? Explain your answers.

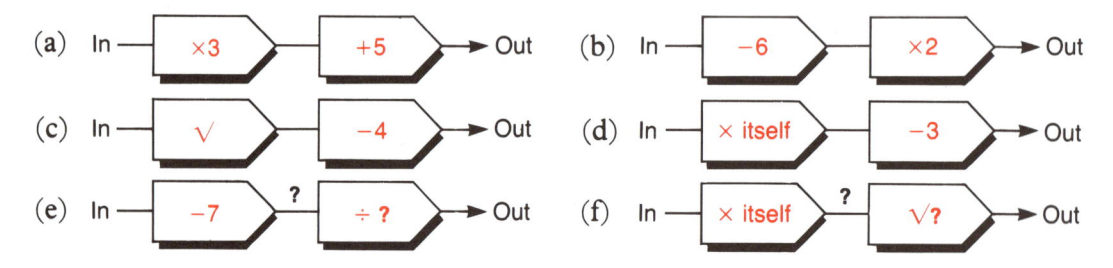

(a) In ⟶ ×3 ⟶ +5 ⟶ Out   (b) In ⟶ −6 ⟶ ×2 ⟶ Out

(c) In ⟶ √ ⟶ −4 ⟶ Out   (d) In ⟶ × itself ⟶ −3 ⟶ Out

(e) In ⟶ −7 ⟶ ÷ ? ⟶ Out   (f) In ⟶ × itself ⟶ √? ⟶ Out

For the rest of this chapter, we shall deal only with function machines.

Look at this function machine.

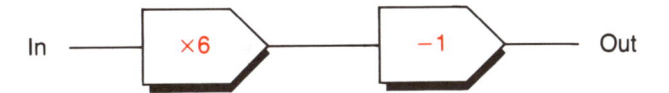

In —[×6]—[−1]— Out

If a goes in, $6a - 1$ comes out:

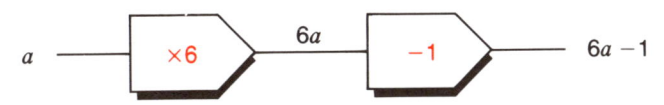

a —[×6]— $6a$ —[−1]— $6a - 1$

A6 Copy and complete each of these chains.

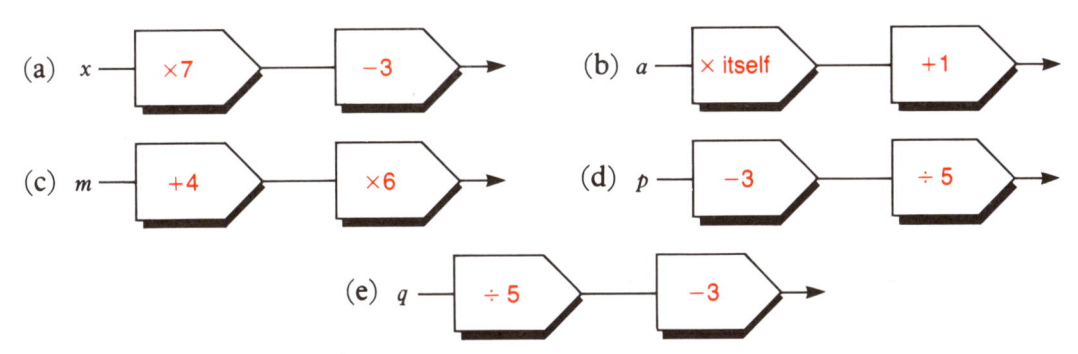

(a) x —[×7]—[−3]→

(b) a —[× itself]—[+1]→

(c) m —[+4]—[×6]→

(d) p —[−3]—[÷5]→

(e) q —[÷5]—[−3]→

B Functional notation

Function machines can be written in a special way.

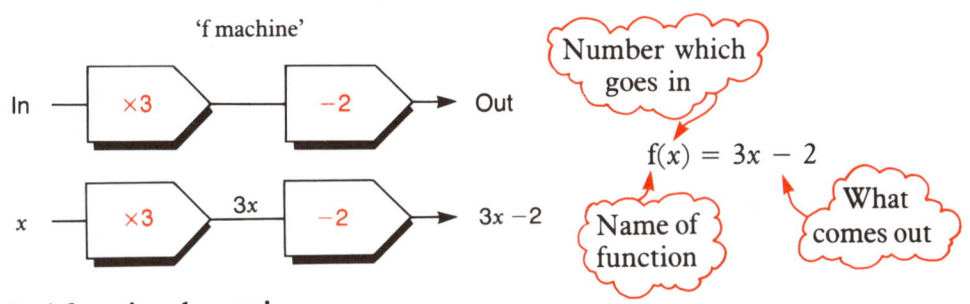

'f machine'

In —[×3]—[−2]→ Out

x —[×3]— $3x$ —[−2]→ $3x - 2$

Number which goes in ↓
$f(x) = 3x - 2$
↑ Name of function
↑ What comes out

This is called **functional notation**.

B1 Re-write each of these chains in functional notation.

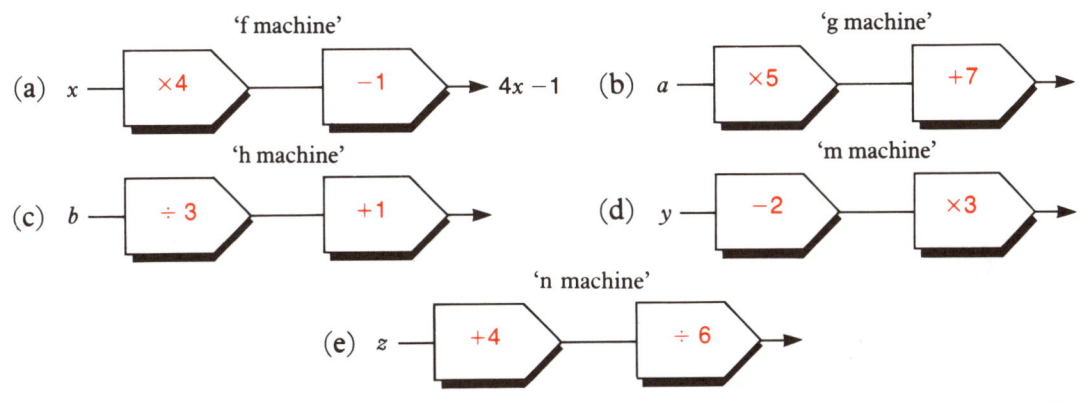

'f machine'
(a) x —[×4]—[−1]→ $4x - 1$

'g machine'
(b) a —[×5]—[+7]→

'h machine'
(c) b —[÷3]—[+1]→

'm machine'
(d) y —[−2]—[×3]→

'n machine'
(e) z —[+4]—[÷6]→

B2 Here are some some functions expressed in words. Re-write them in functional notation.

The first one has been started for you.

(a) Multiply by 2, then subtract 7.

$f(x) = 2x \ldots$

(b) Multiply by itself, then add 7.

(c) Add 1, then multiply by 2.

(d) Multiply by itself, subtract 7, then multiply by 3.

B3 Here are some functions written in functional notation.

Re-write them in words.

(a) $f(x) = x + 7$ (b) $g(x) = 4 - x^2$ (c) $g(y) = \dfrac{y^2 - 6}{2}$

(d) $h(z) = 3z^2 - 1$ (e) $b(a) = 9(a^2 + 2)$

C Evaluations

We can use functional notation to evaluate a function for any number. For example,

'f machine'

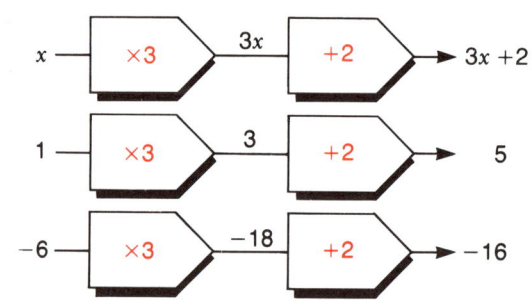

$x \to [\times 3] \to 3x \to [+2] \to 3x + 2 \qquad f(x) = 3x + 2$

$1 \to [\times 3] \to 3 \to [+2] \to 5 \qquad f(1) = (3 \times 1) + 2 = 5$

$-6 \to [\times 3] \to -18 \to [+2] \to -16 \qquad f(-6) = (3 \times -6) + 2 = -16$

C1 If $f(x) = 4x - 5$, evaluate

(a) $f(5)$ (b) $f(0)$ (c) $f(-3)$

C2 If $g(y) = 7 - 2y$, evaluate

(a) $g(1)$ (b) $g(8)$ (c) $g(-2)$

C3 If $h(x) = x^2 + 2$, evaluate

(a) $h(0)$ (b) $h(4)$ (c) $h(-1)$

If we put a machine chain into reverse, we can find out what number went in. Here is an example.

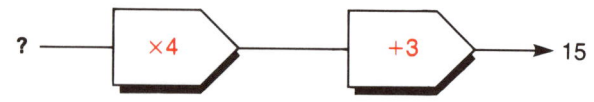

$? \to [\times 4] \to [+3] \to 15$

We can undo the machine like this:

3 ← [÷ 4] ← 12 ← [− 3] ← 15   3 went in.

We can do the same thing using functional notation. For example,

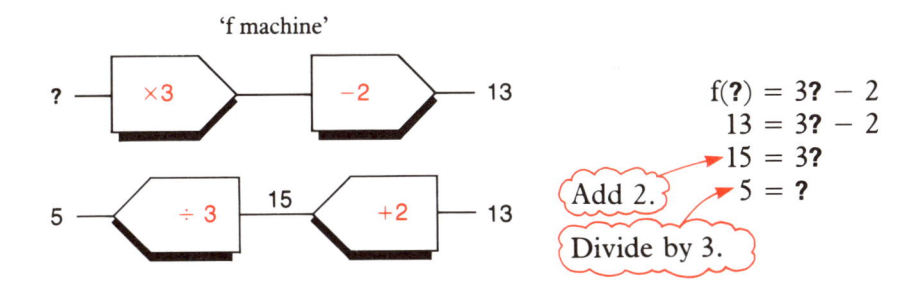

'f machine'

? → [×3] → [−2] → 13

5 → [÷ 3] → 15 → [+2] → 13

$f(?) = 3? − 2$
$13 = 3? − 2$
$15 = 3?$
$5 = ?$

Add 2.
Divide by 3.

C4 Work out the value of the **?** in each of the following.

(a) $f(x) = 2x + 1$
    $f(?) = 7$

(b) $g(x) = 5x − 7$
    $g(?) = 42$

(c) $p(y) = 9 − 2y$
    $p(?) = 27$

(d) $q(z) = \dfrac{z}{7}$
    $q(?) = 8$

D Linear functions

When we have to evaluate a function for several values, it is easier to set out the answers in a table, like this.

x	1	2	3	4	5	6
$f(x)$						

Worked example

Evaluate the function $f(x) = 3x + 2$ for $1 \leq x \leq 6$ (that is, for $x = 1, 2, 3, 4, 5$ and 6).

If $x = 1$, $f(x) = (3 \times 1) + 2 = 5$
If $x = 2$, $f(x) = (3 \times 2) + 2 = 8$
If $x = 3$, $f(x) = (3 \times 3) + 2 = 11$
If $x = 4$, $f(x) = (3 \times 4) + 2 = 14$
If $x = 5$, $f(x) = (3 \times 5) + 2 = 17$
If $x = 6$, $f(x) = (3 \times 6) + 2 = 20$

x	1	2	3	4	5	6
$3x + 2$	5	8	11	14	17	20

D1 Make up a table like the one in the worked example and evaluate each of the given functions. Use the values of x that are stated.

The first one has been started for you.

(a) $f(x) = 4x - 1 \qquad 1 \leq x \leq 6$

x	1	2		5	
$f(x)$	3		15		

(b) $g(x) = 3 + 2x \qquad 0 \leq x \leq 6$
(c) $h(x) = 3 - 6x \qquad 0 \leq x \leq 5$
(d) $p(x) = 2(1 + 2x) \qquad 1 \leq x \leq 5$
(e) $v(x) = \frac{3}{2}x - 1 \qquad 0 \leq x \leq 5$
(f) $q(x) = \frac{1}{2} - 4x \qquad 0 \leq x \leq 5$

Graphs

Sometimes Fussy Flo fills her bath too full, and the water overflows when she gets in.

If the bath were this shape then the water level would rise at a constant rate as Flo got into the bath.

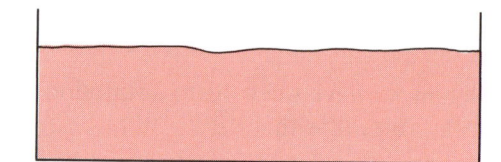

We can think of this as a function. The input is the time Flo takes to get into the bath and the output is the depth of water in the bath.

So if the depth of water at time t is $d(t)$, then the graph of this depth function might look like this.

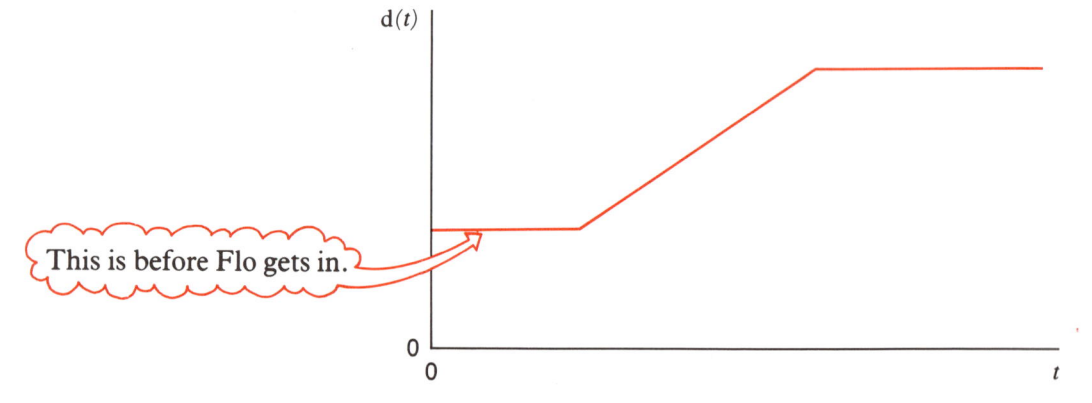

This is before Flo gets in.

D2 Here is a different shape of bath.

Draw a sketch showing the general shape of the function d(*t*).

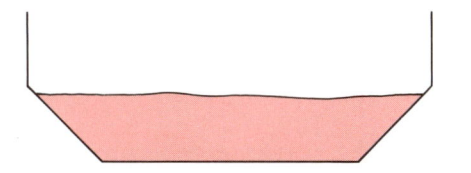

D3 Repeat question D2 for each of these baths.

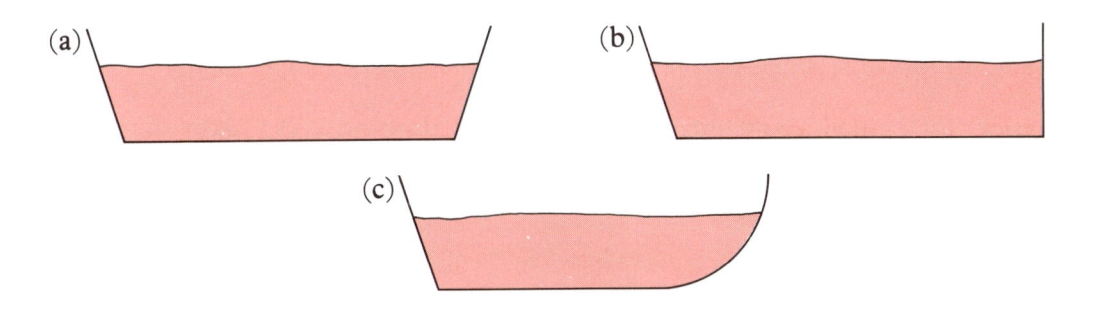

(a)

(b)

(c)

D4 Here is the graph of the depth function of another bath.

From the graph, give as much information about the bath as you can.

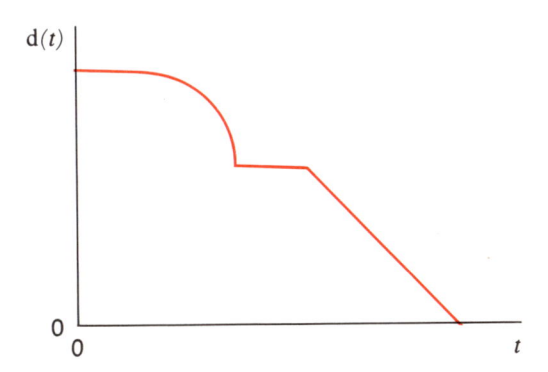

When we evaluated the function $f(x) = 3x + 2$ in the worked example, we obtained the table of values below.

x	1	2	3	4	5	6
$f(x)$	5	8	11	14	17	20

We can plot these values as points on a graph.

The x-values are the x-coordinates (on the horizontal axis) and the $f(x)$ values are the y-coordinates (on the vertical axis).

So the points are

(1, 5), (2, 8), (3, 11), (4, 14), (5, 17) and (6, 20).

If we join up the points, we obtain the graph of the function $f(x) = 3x + 2$.

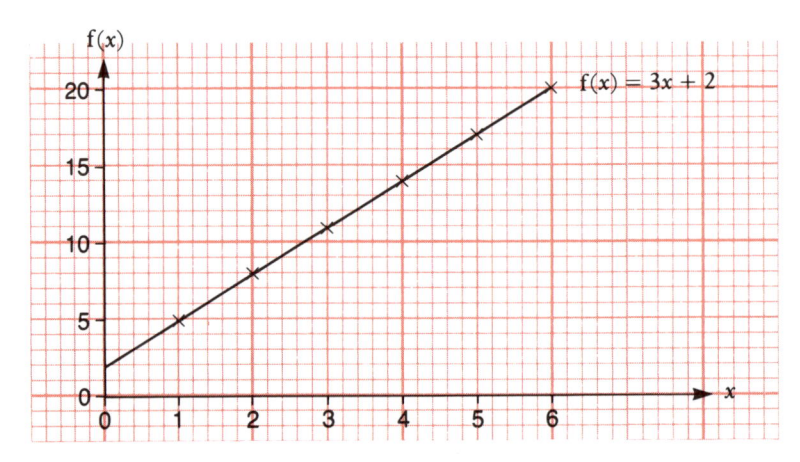

Since its graph is a straight line, we call $f(x)$ a **linear function**.

D5 Make up a table of values for each of the following functions, and hence draw their graphs.

Use the values of x that are stated, and use scales of 1 cm for one unit on both axes.

(a) $f(x) = 4x + 3$ $0 \leqslant x \leqslant 5$

(b) $g(x) = 3x - 1$ $0 \leqslant x \leqslant 5$

(c) $c(x) = 5 - x$ $0 \leqslant x \leqslant 5$

(d) $h(x) = 1 - 2x$ $-4 \leqslant x \leqslant 2$

(e) $p(x) = 4(x - 2)$ $-3 \leqslant x \leqslant 2$

(f) $q(x) = \frac{1}{2}x + 2$ $-2 \leqslant x \leqslant 4$

E Quadratic functions

Functions that have a 'squared' term as their term with the highest power are called **quadratic** functions.

For example, $f(x) = x^2 + 3x + 9$

and $f(x) = 2x^2 - 4$ are quadratic functions.

But $f(x) = 2x^3 + 3x^2 + 9$ is *not* a quadratic function.

In general form, $f(x) = ax^2 + bx + c$ defines a quadratic function, so long as $a \neq 0$.

E1 Which of the following are quadratic functions?

(a) $g(x) = 3x^2 + 9x - 4$ (b) $f(x) = x^3 - 2x^2 + 3$

(c) $p(x) = 2x + 4$ (d) $m(x) = 14 - 3x^2$

(e) $v(x) = x^2$ (f) $z(x) = x^2 - x^3$

F Evaluating quadratic functions

When we have to evaluate a quadratic function, it is helpful to use a table, as before. We can then use the information from the table to draw a graph of the function.

Worked example

If $f(x) = x^2 + x - 2$, find $f(-3), f(-2), f(-1), f(0), f(1), f(2)$ and $f(3)$.

Use this information to draw the graph of $f(x)$ for $-3 \leq x \leq 3$.

1 Draw a table splitting up the terms of the function.

$f(x) = x^2 + x - 2$

x	−3	−2	−1	0	1	2	3
x^2							
$+x$							
-2							
$f(x)$							

Terms of the function.

Add the terms together to evaluate the function.

2 Complete the table.

x	−3	−2	−1	0	1	2	3
x^2	9	4	1	0	1	4	9
$+x$	−3	−2	−1	0	1	2	3
-2	−2	−2	−2	−2	−2	−2	−2
$f(x)$	4	0	−2	−2	0	4	10

3 List the points.

(−3, 4), (−2, 0), (−1, −2),

(0, −2), (1, 0), (2, 4),

(3, 10)

4 Draw suitable axes.

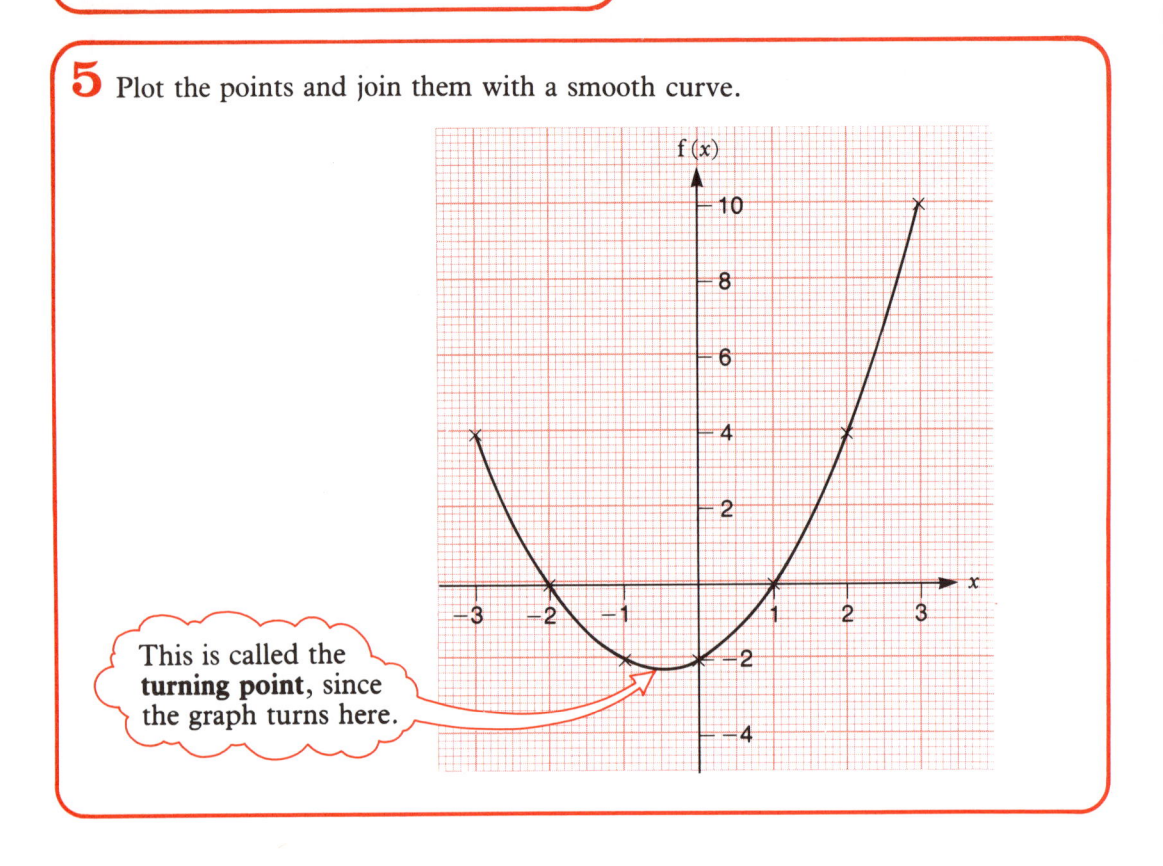

5 Plot the points and join them with a smooth curve.

*This is called the **turning point**, since the graph turns here.*

The shape of this graph is called a **parabola**.

Here are some examples for you to try.

F1 (a) Copy and complete the table below for the function
$f(x) = x^2 - 2x - 8$ for $-2 \leq x \leq 6$.

x	−2	−1	0	1	2	3	4	5	6
x^2									
$-2x$									
-8									
$f(x)$									

(b) From your table, list the points which lie on the graph of $f(x) = x^2 - 2x - 8$ for $-2 \leq x \leq 6$.

(c) Draw suitable axes on 5 mm squared paper and complete the graph of $f(x) = x^2 - 2x - 8$ for $-2 \leq x \leq 6$.

F2 (a) Copy and complete the table below for the function
$f(x) = x^2 - 2x - 3$ for $-3 \leqslant x \leqslant 4$.

x	-3	-2	-1	0	1	2	3	4
x^2								
$-2x$								
-3								
$f(x)$								

(b) From your table, list the points which lie on the graph of
$f(x) = x^2 - 2x - 3$ for $-3 \leqslant x \leqslant 4$.

(c) Draw suitable axes on 5 mm squared paper and complete the graph of $f(x) = x^2 - 2x - 3$ for $-3 \leqslant x \leqslant 4$.

F3 (a) Copy and complete the table below for the function $f(x) = 9 - x^2$ for $-4 \leqslant x \leqslant 4$.

x	-4	-3	-2						
9									
$-x^2$									
$f(x)$									

(b) From your table, list the points which lie on the graph of the function.

(c) Draw suitable axes on 5 mm squared paper and complete the graph of $f(x) = 9 - x^2$ for $-4 \leqslant x \leqslant 4$.

F4 (a) Use a table to evaluate the function $f(x) = -x^2 - x + 2$ for $-3 \leqslant x \leqslant 2$.

(b) List the points which will lie on the graph.

(c) Draw suitable axes on 5 mm squared paper and complete the graph of $f(x) = -x^2 - x + 2$ for $-3 \leqslant x \leqslant 2$.

F5 (a) Use a table to evaluate the function $f(x) = -2x^2 + 7x - 6$ for $-1 \leqslant x \leqslant 3$.

(b) List the points which will lie on the graph.

(c) Draw the graph of $f(x) = -2x^2 + 7x - 6$ for $-1 \leqslant x \leqslant 3$ on 5 mm squared paper.

F6 (a) Use a table to evaluate the function $f(x) = 2x^2 + 3x + 3$ for $-2 \leq x \leq 2$.

(b) List the points which will lie on the graph.

(c) Draw the graph of the function on 5 mm squared paper.

F7 Look at the graphs of the functions with 'positive' x^2 terms, and describe their shape.

F8 Look at the graphs of the functions with 'negative' x^2 terms, and describe their shape.

The values of x which make the function equal to zero are called the **zeros** or **roots** of the equation.

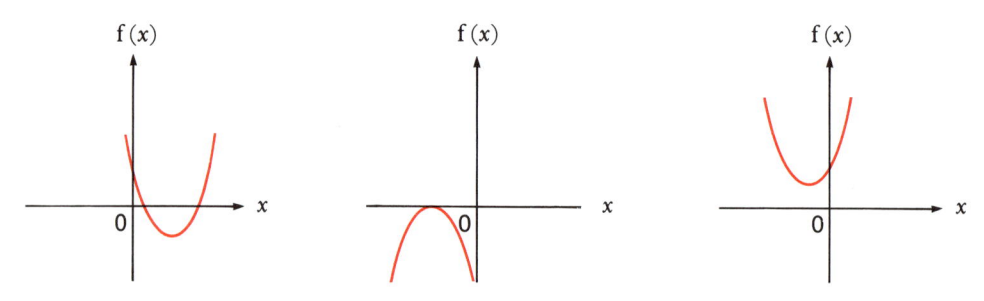

This graph has two roots.   This graph has one root.   This graph has no roots.

F9 List the roots of the functions in questions F1 to F6 (where they exist).

Write your answers like this.

> F9 $f(x) = x^2 - 2x - 8$
> Roots at $x = 4$ and $x = -2$
>
> $f(x) = x^2 - 2x - 3$
> Roots at $x =$

F10 Explain whereabouts on its graph you would find the roots of a quadratic equation.

F11 Look at the graph of the function $f(x) = x^2 - 2x - 8$ from question F1.

It has roots at $x = 4$ and $x = -2$.

(a) Does this graph have a turning point at its highest point or its lowest point?

(b) Would you call this a 'maximum turning point' or a 'minimum turning point'?

(c) What is the value of the function at the turning point? (This is called the **turning value** of the function.)

(d) What value of x gives this value?

(e) Explain how you would work out this value of x from the roots of the function.

F12 Copy and complete the table below for the functions in questions F2 to F6.

One of them has been done for you.

Function	Maximum or minimum turning point?	Turning value	Coordinates of turning point
$f(x) = x^2 - 2x - 3$			
$f(x) = 9 - x^2$			
$f(x) = -x^2 - x + 2$	Maximum	$2\frac{1}{4}$	$(\frac{1}{2}, 2\frac{1}{4})$
$f(x) = -2x^2 + 7x - 6$			
$f(x) = 2x^2 + 3x + 3$			

As these numbers are not whole numbers, we approximate them from the graph.

G Investigation

Here are the graphs of three quadratic functions.

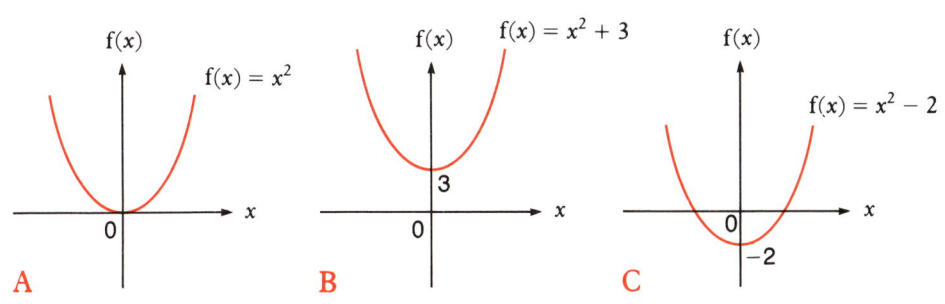

A: $f(x) = x^2$

B: $f(x) = x^2 + 3$

C: $f(x) = x^2 - 2$

Trace graph A.

Check that your tracing fits over graphs B and C.

To get graph B from graph A we would move graph A three units upwards.

Explain how you could get graph C from graph A.

How could you get graph C from graph B?

How could the graph of $f(x) = x^2 + 7$ be moved onto the graph of $f(x) = x^2 - 4$? (Don't draw the graphs.)

Investigate further how the equation changes as graph A is moved to other positions.

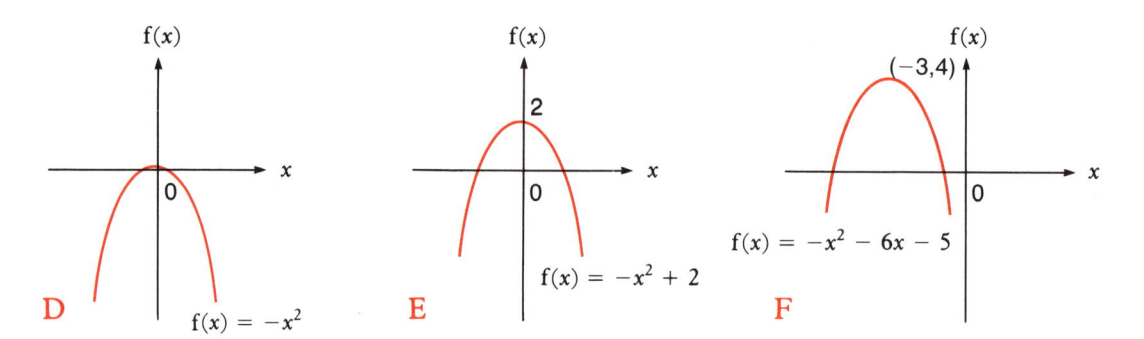

D $f(x) = -x^2$

E $f(x) = -x^2 + 2$

F $f(x) = -x^2 - 6x - 5$, vertex $(-3, 4)$

Take your tracing of graph A and check that it also fits over graphs D, E and F.

Investigate how the equation changes as graph A takes up these different positions.

Explain how you could fit graph D over graph E.

How could you get

    (a)   graph D from graph A

    (b)   graph F from graph A (there are two ways to do this – find both of them)

    (c)   graph D from graph B (find two ways of doing this also)

Look at the equations of graphs A and D. Also look at the equations of graphs C and E.

What do you notice about the graphs and the equations?

What would be the equation of the function whose graph was like graph B upside-down?

What would be the equation of the function whose graph was like graph F upside-down?

H Making the most of it

Quadratic functions can sometimes help us to solve problems in everyday life.

Worked example

Digger Matt set out to stake his claim to a piece of ground on which to search for gold. He was told that he could have as much ground as he could enclose into a rectangle by using 50 m of fencing.

How could Matt ensure that he had enclosed the largest possible area?

What would this area be?

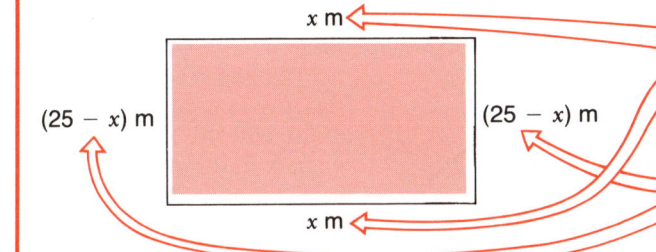

1 Form the information into a function.

Let the length be x m.

Then each breadth will be $(25 - x)$ m.

The rectangle has length x m (top and bottom) and breadth $(25 - x)$ m (left and right sides).

$$\begin{aligned} \text{Area of rectangle} &= \text{Length} \times \text{Breadth} \\ &= x(25 - x) \text{ m}^2 \\ &= (25x - x^2) \text{ m}^2 \end{aligned}$$

Function is $A(x) = 25x - x^2$

We call the function $A(x)$ because it is measuring Area.

2 Evaluate the function for suitable values of x.

We shall go up in fives. (The other values will be found later from the graph.)

x	0	5	10	15	20	25
$25x$	0	125	250	375	500	625
$-x^2$	0	-25	-100	-225	-400	-625
$A(x)$	0	100	150	150	100	0

3 List the points from the table.

(0, 0), (5, 100), (10, 150), (15, 150), (20, 100), (25, 0)

There is no point in looking at values of x bigger than 25 or less than 0. They would give a negative area, which is impossible.

4 Draw the graph of the function on 2 mm graph paper.

Use the graph to find which value of x gives the greatest area, and what this area is.

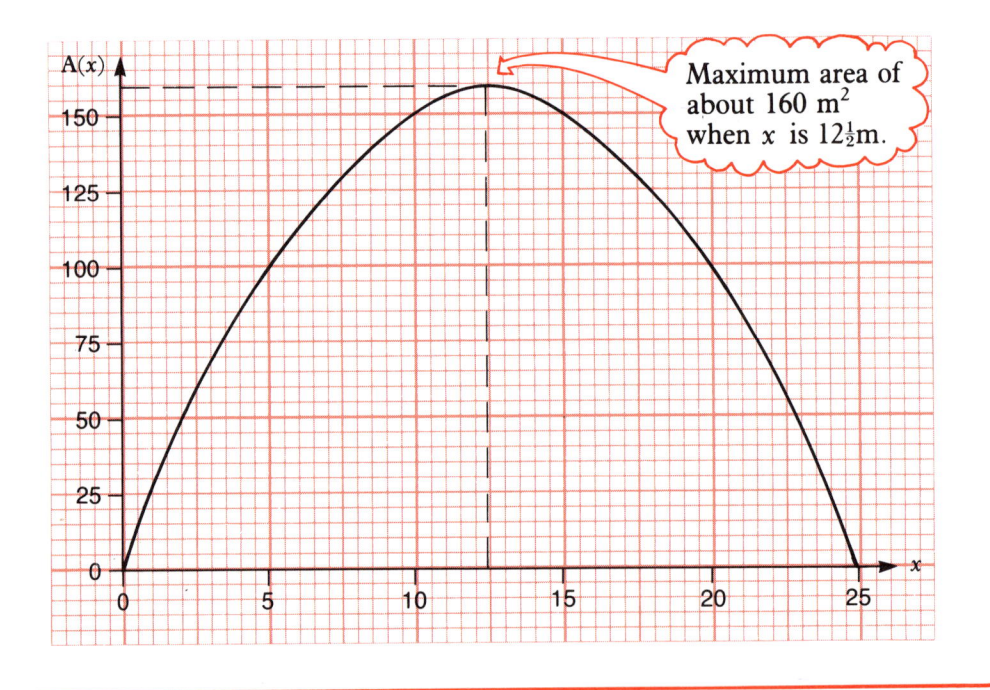

Maximum area of about 160 m² when x is $12\frac{1}{2}$ m.

Here are some examples for you to try.

H1 Matt's friend, Peter Gold, had only 40 m of fencing with which to stake his claim.

(a) Form a function for the area of the rectangle that Peter could fence in.

(b) Work out the values of the function for $0 \leq x \leq 20$. (Go up in fours.)

(c) Use this information to draw the graph of the function for $0 \leqslant x \leqslant 20$ on 2 mm graph paper.

(d) Use the graph to work out what value of *x* would give the greatest area, and what the greatest area would be.

H2 Peter's cousin Mary had 50 m of fencing to stake her rectangular claim, next to the river.

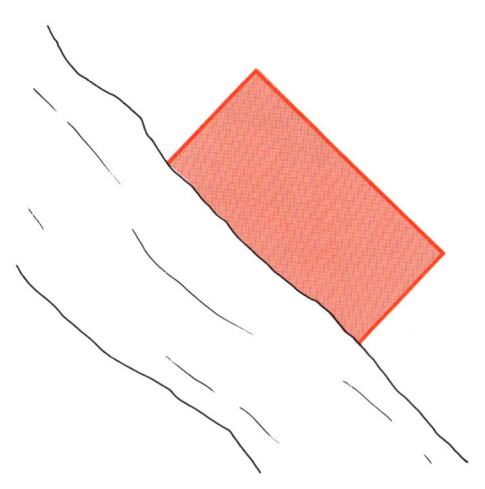

(a) Form a function for the area of Mary's plot of land.

(b) Work out the values of the function for $0 \leqslant x \leqslant 25$. (Go up in fives.)

(c) Use this information to draw the graph of the function for $0 \leqslant x \leqslant 25$ on 2 mm graph paper.

(d) What is the greatest area of ground that Mary could claim?

H3 Wilma is building a rectangular run for her rabbit using 10 m of wire netting. She wants the run to have as large an area as possible.

She can build the run in the middle of the garden or against a wall.

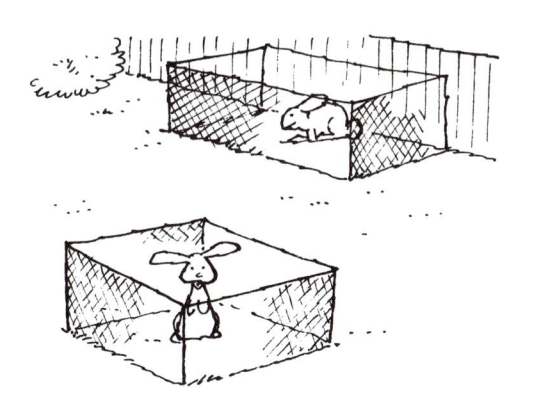

Which position will give the rabbit the biggest run?

What will the dimensions and area of this run be?

H4 A short-range ballistic missile has been set up to shoot at a target 450 m away. The missile's path is determined by the rule $h(t) = 420t - t^2$, where h(*t*) is its height above the ground at time *t* seconds after it is launched.

By drawing a graph of h(*t*), determine whether or not the missile will reach the target.

H5 This plane is flying between Gatwick and Beauvais in France.
Its flight-path is determined by the rule $h(m) = 750m - 25m^2$, where $h(m)$ is its height in metres at time m minutes after taking off from Gatwick.

Use a graph to determine

(a) the height at which the aircraft begins its descent

(b) how long the flight takes

I Cubic functions

Functions that have a 'cubed' term as their term with the highest power are called **cubic** functions.

For example, $f(x) = 2x^3 + 9$
and $f(x) = 9x^3 + 2x^2 + 3x - 4$ *are* cubic functions.
But $f(x) = x^4 - x^3$
and $f(x) = 9x^5 - 2x^3 - 2x - 4$ are *not* cubic functions.

In general form, $f(x) = ax^3 + bx^2 + cx + d$ defines a cubic function, so long as $a \neq 0$.

We can evaluate cubic functions in the same way as we did quadratic functions, by using a table.

Worked example

Evaluate $f(x) = x^3 - x^2 - 2x$ for $-3 \leq x \leq 3$.

Draw the graph of $f(x)$ on graph paper.

Use the graph to write down the roots of the function.

1 Draw a table and complete it.

x	-3	-2	-1	0	1	2	3
x^3	-27	-8	-1	0	1	8	27
$-x^2$	-9	-4	-1	0	-1	-4	-9
$-2x$	6	4	2	0	-2	-4	-6
$f(x)$	-30	-8	0	0	-2	0	12

2 List the points.

$(-3, -30), (-2, -8), (-1, 0), (0, 0), (1, -2), (2, 0), (3, 12)$

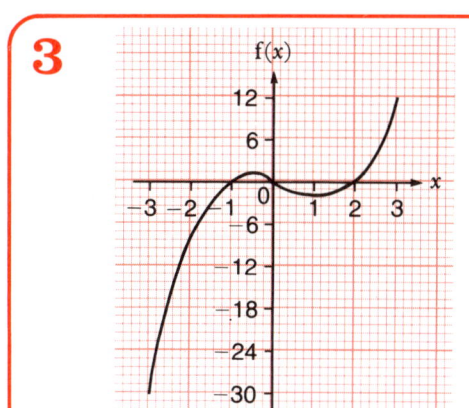

3 Draw suitable axes. Plot the points and join them with a smooth curve.

4 List the roots.

Roots are at $x = -1$, $x = 0$ and $x = 2$.

Here are some examples for you to try.

I1 Let $f(x) = x^3 - 8x^2 + 15x$.

(a) Evaluate $f(x)$ for $-1 \leqslant x \leqslant 6$.

(b) Draw the graph of $f(x)$ for $-1 \leqslant x \leqslant 6$.

(c) Use your graph to write down the roots of the function.

I2 Let $f(x) = x^3 - 2x^2 - 5x + 6$.

(a) Evaluate $f(x)$ for $-3 \leqslant x \leqslant 4$.

(b) Draw the graph of $f(x)$ for $-3 \leqslant x \leqslant 4$.

(c) Write down the roots of $f(x)$.

13 Let $f(x) = 2x^3 + 3x^2 - 3x - 2$.

(a) Evaluate $f(x)$ for $-3 \leq x \leq 2$.

(b) Draw the graph of $f(x)$ for $-3 \leq x \leq 2$.

(c) Write down the roots of $f(x)$.

14 Let $f(x) = -x^3 + x^2 + 14x - 24$.

(a) Evaluate $f(x)$ for $-5 \leq x \leq 3$.

(b) Draw the graph of $f(x)$ for $-5 \leq x \leq 3$.

(c) Write down the roots of $f(x)$.

15 Let $f(x) = -2x^3 + 10x^2 - 4x - 16$.

(a) Evaluate $f(x)$ for $-2 \leq x \leq 5$.

(b) Draw the graph of $f(x)$ for $-2 \leq x \leq 5$.

(c) Write down the roots of $f(x)$.

J Making the best of it

Like quadratic functions, cubic functions can sometimes help us to solve problems in everyday life.

Worked example

Chocko Ltd wants to make open boxes for its chocolates from sheets of cardboard 30 cm by 30 cm as shown here.

They want to make sure that the boxes hold as many chocolates as possible.

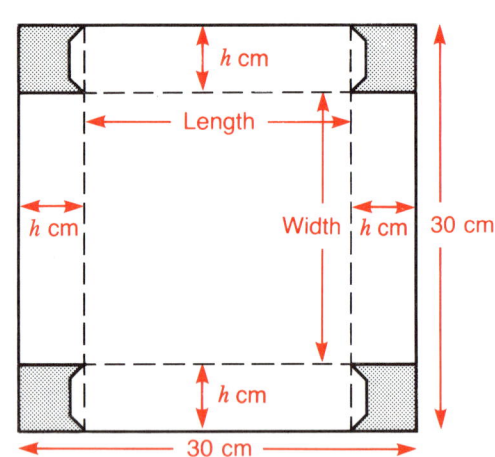

If the height of the box is h cm, write down expressions for the length and the width of the box.

Form a function $V(h)$ for the volume of the box.

Evaluate the function for $0 \leq h \leq 14$. (Go up in twos.)

Draw the graph of the function for $0 \leq h \leq 14$.

Use your graph to estimate the dimensions of the box with the greatest volume, and what this volume will be.

1 Write down expressions.

Length = $30 - 2h$
Width = $30 - 2h$
Height = h

2 Work out the volume.

Volume = Length × Width × Height
$= (30 - 2h)(30 - 2h)h$
$= (900 - 120h + 4h^2)h$
$= 900h - 120h^2 + 4h^3$
$V(h) = 900h - 120h^2 + 4h^3$

3 Evaluate the function.

h	0	2	4	6	8	10	12	14
$900h$	0	1800	3600	5400	7200	9000	10800	12600
$-120h^2$	0	-480	-1920	-4320	-7680	-12000	-17280	-23520
$4h^3$	0	32	256	864	2048	4000	6912	10976
$V(h)$	0	1352	1936	1944	1568	1000	432	56

4 List the points from the table.

(0, 0), (2, 1352), (4, 1936), (6, 1944), (8, 1568), (10, 1000), (12, 432), (14, 56)

5 Draw suitable axes. Plot the points and join them with a smooth curve.

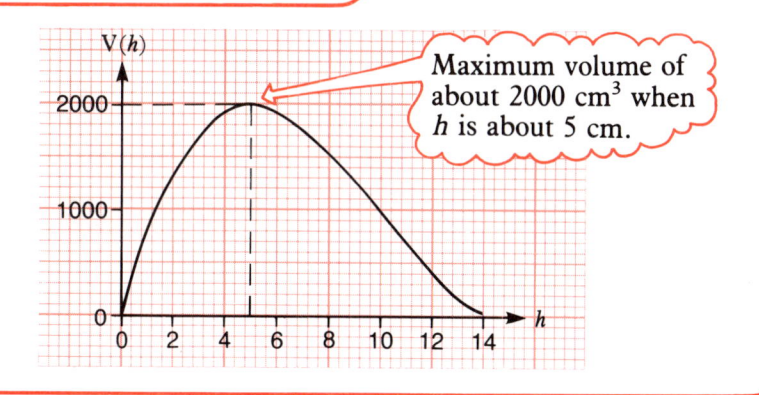

Maximum volume of about 2000 cm³ when h is about 5 cm.

J1 Here are some examples for you to try.

Yummy Chocs Ltd sells its chocolates in open cartons made from sheets of cardboard 30 cm by 20 cm to this pattern.

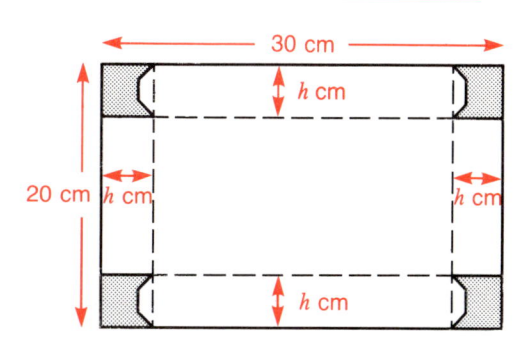

(a) If the height of the box is h cm, write down expressions for the length and the width of the box.

(b) Form a function $V(h)$ for the volume of the box.

(c) Evaluate the function for $h = 0, 2, 4, 6, 8$ and 10.

(d) Draw the graph $V(h)$ for $0 \leq h \leq 10$ on 2 mm graph paper.

(e) From your graph, estimate the dimensions of the carton with the greatest volume, and what this volume will be.

J2 Le Choc Chocolates are sold in lidded boxes made from sheets of card 20 cm by 50 cm cut to the pattern below.

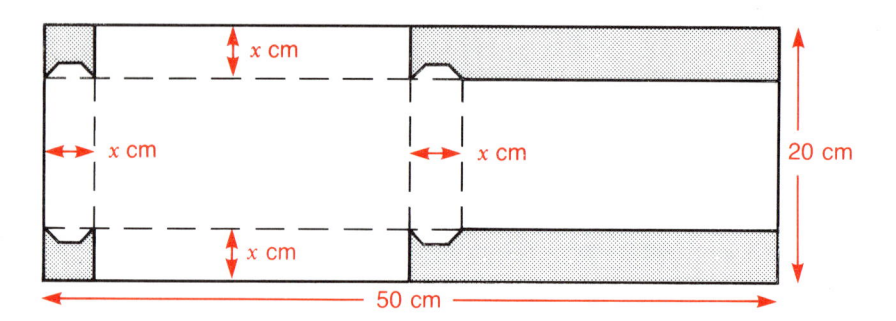

(a) If the height of the box is x cm, write down expressions for the length and the width of the box.

(b) Form a function $V(x)$ for the volume of the box.

(c) Evaluate $V(x)$ for $1 \leq x \leq 8$.

(d) Draw a graph of $V(x)$ for $1 \leq x \leq 8$ on 2 mm graph paper.

(e) Use your graph to estimate the dimensions of the box with the greatest volume, and what this volume will be.

Money management 3: hire purchase and VAT

A Hire purchase

Now Cathy has a regular income, she can afford to buy larger items, and she has decided to buy herself a stereo unit.

She does not want to use up all her savings to do this, but wants to 'pay it up' from her wages every week. This is called **hire purchase**. Sometimes shops charge extra for purchases made in this way. The extra charge is called **interest**.

The hire purchase price of the washing machine can be worked out like this:

Payments = 10 × £22·50 = £225·00
Interest   = 15% of £250 =   £37·50
                    Total = £262·50

Superb Offer! WASHING MACHINE £250 or 10 weeks at £22·50 + 15% interest on cash price

A1 Cathy has chosen the stereo unit she wants, and she has seen it in a number of places. Help Cathy choose which of the places will give her the best deal by working out how much she will pay in each of them.

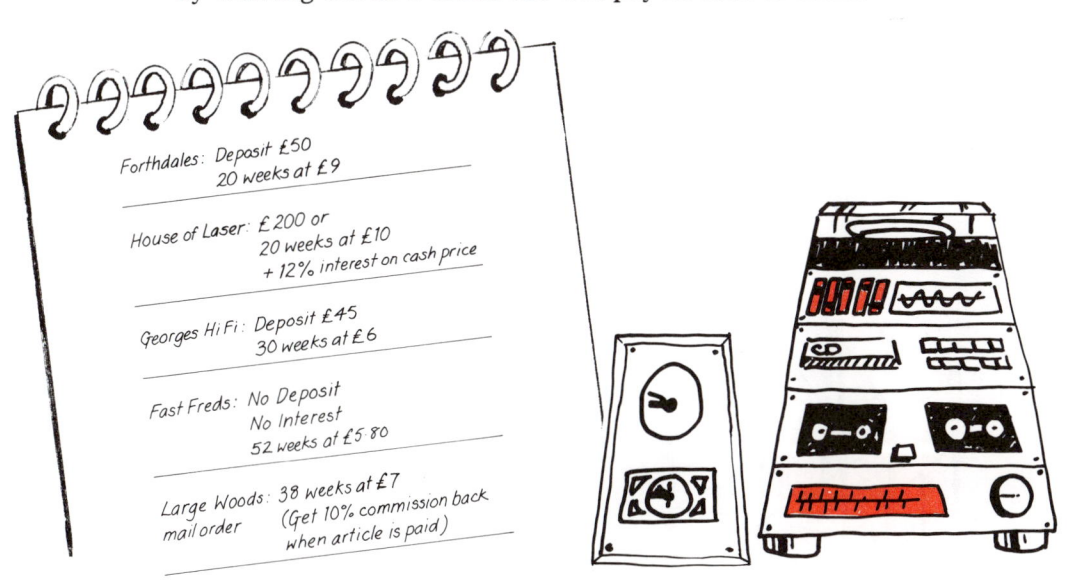

Forthdales: Deposit £50
           20 weeks at £9

House of Laser: £200 or
               20 weeks at £10
               + 12% interest on cash price

Georges Hi Fi: Deposit £45
              30 weeks at £6

Fast Freds: No Deposit
           No Interest
           52 weeks at £5·80

Large Woods: 38 weeks at £7
mail order   (Get 10% commission back
             when article is paid)

Here are some more questions about hire purchase.

A2 The cash price of this knitting machine is £239·95.

It can also be bought by 'paying it up' for 100 weeks at £2·96 per week.

(a) Work out the total hire purchase price.

(b) How much more than the cash price is this?

(c) Work out the interest as a percentage of the cash price, to the nearest whole number.

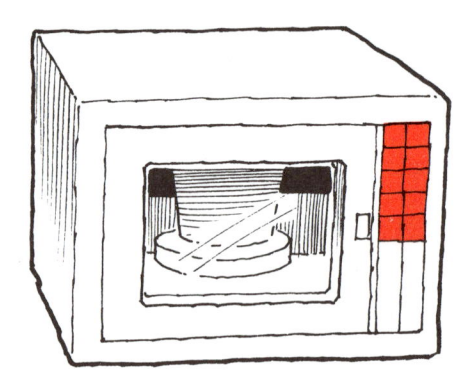

A3 The cash price of this microwave oven is £220.

The hire purchase terms are 75 weeks at £3·25.

(a) Calculate the total hire purchase price.

(b) Work out the interest as a percentage of the cash price, to the nearest whole number.

A4 The hire purchase price of this fridge freezer is £315·40, including 17% interest.

(a) If payments are to be made for 50 weeks, work out the cost per week.

(b) Work out the cash price of the freezer.

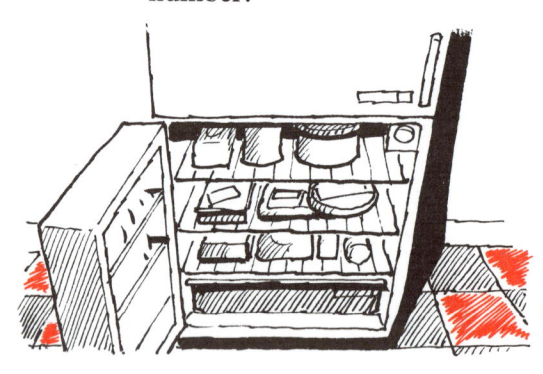

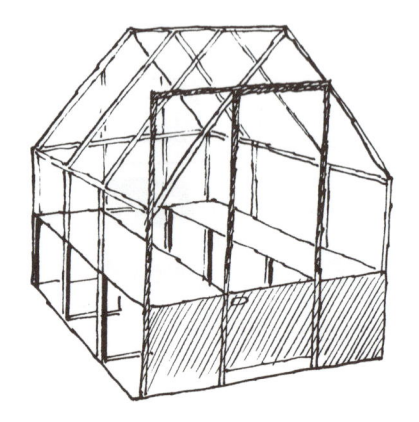

A5 The cash price of this greenhouse is £179·99.

It can also be bought on hire purchase by paying a deposit of £50 and 50 payments of £3·65.

Calculate how much extra is paid if the greenhouse is bought on hire purchase.

A6 This three-piece suite has a cash price of £499·99.

It can also be bought under three different hire purchase schemes:

A 10% deposit and 52 payments of £9·76
B Deposit of £75 and 35 payments of £14·57
C No deposit and 105 payments of £5·17

Which scheme charges the least interest?

A7 This fitted kitchen's cash price is £1265.

It can be bought over a period of a year if a deposit of £100 is made, the balance being subject to interest at 29·6%.

Calculate the monthly payments which would be charged.

B VAT

Colin was visiting a warehouse to collect things for his work. He saw Cathy's stereo unit there with this price tag on it.

£199 + VAT

He thought Cathy would be annoyed when he told her about this, but she just laughed and said

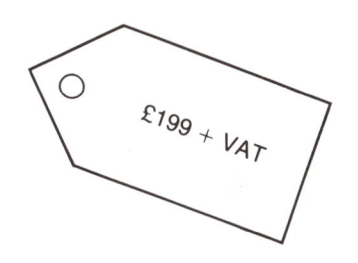

> The warehouse price has no Value Added Tax in it, Colin. The prices in the shops included VAT. So we must add on the tax to the warehouse price before comparing prices. The rate of VAT is 15% at the moment. 15% of £199 is just under £30, so the price is about £229. I've still got a good bargain!

B1 Here are some more price tags which do not include VAT. Work out the cost of each item including VAT.

The first one has been started for you.

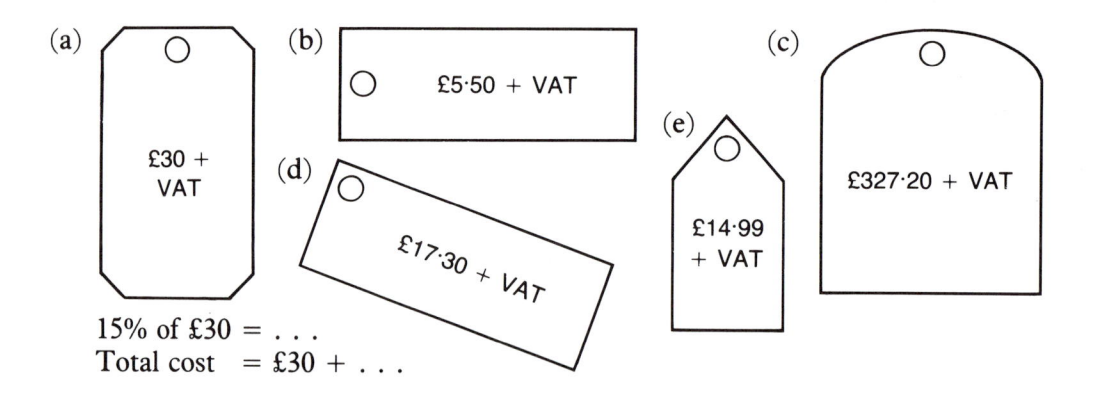

(a) £30 + VAT
(b) £5·50 + VAT
(c) £327·20 + VAT
(d) £17·30 + VAT
(e) £14·99 + VAT

15% of £30 = . . .
Total cost = £30 + . . .

B2 These price tags do include VAT. Work out the cost of each item *before* tax.

The first one has been done for you.

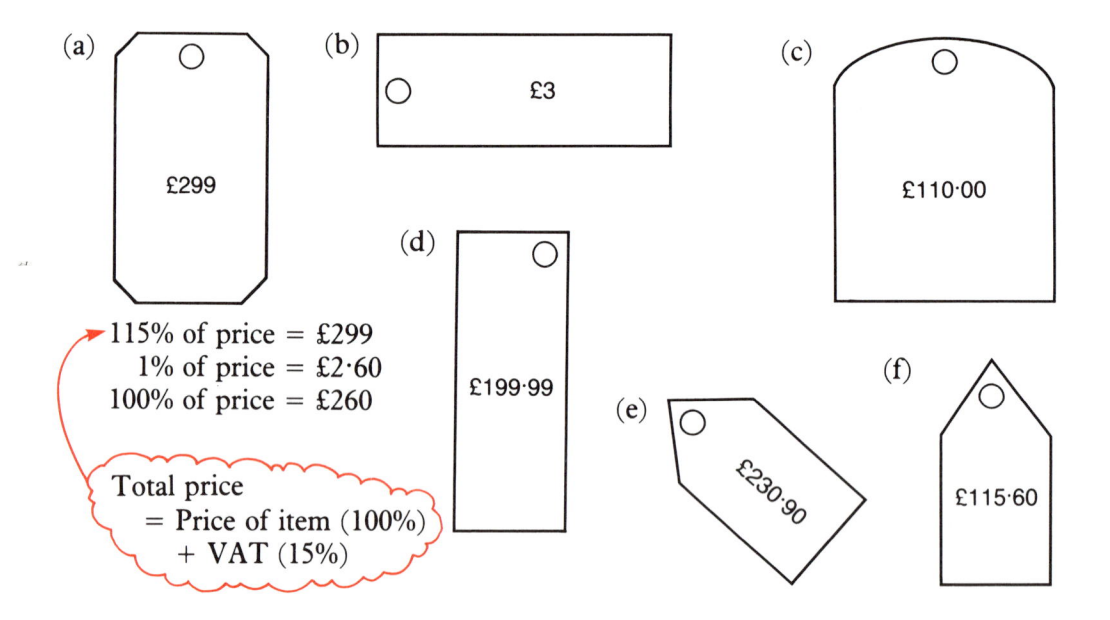

(a) £299
(b) £3
(c) £110·00
(d) £199·99
(e) £230·90
(f) £115·60

115% of price = £299
1% of price = £2·60
100% of price = £260

Total price
 = Price of item (100%)
 + VAT (15%)

5 Angles greater than 90°

A The trundle wheel

A trundle wheel like this can be used to measure distances.

As it rotates, the mark on the circumference moves round like this:

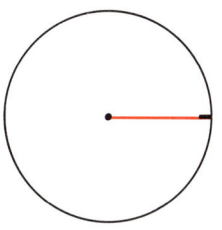

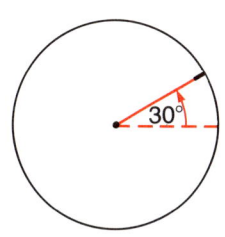

At the start   30° from the start   60° from the start   180° from the start

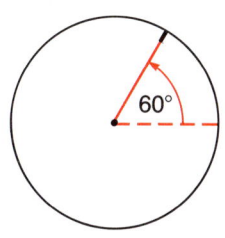

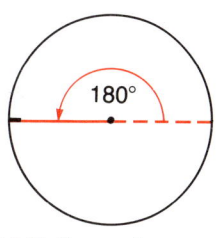

A1 Sketch the wheel as it looks
(a) 90° (b) 150° (c) 270° (d) 360° from the start.

The distance of the mark above or below the starting point also changes as the wheel turns:

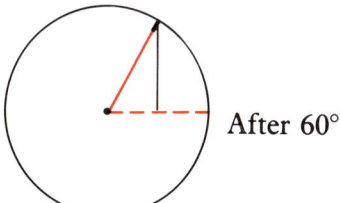

After 60° 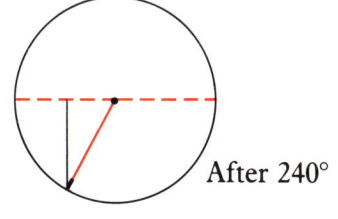   After 240°

We can use trigonometry to calculate the distance of the mark above the starting point.

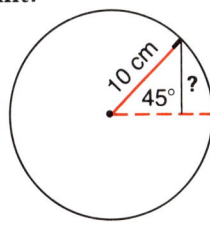

$$\sin 45° = \frac{?}{10}$$
$$? = 10 \sin 45°$$
$$? = 7\cdot07 \text{ cm}$$

65

A2 This diagram shows the wheel after a turn of 240°.

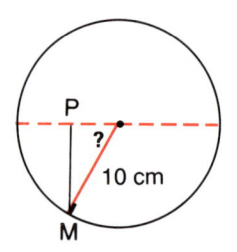

(a) What size is the angle marked?

(b) Calculate the distance, MP, of the mark below the starting point.

A3 Copy and complete this table for a wheel with 10 cm radius.

Degrees from start	Above or below?	Distance MP
0		0 cm
30		
60		
90		
120		
150		
180		
210		
240	Below	8.7 cm
⋮		
360		

A4 Use the table from question A3 to complete this graph of (degrees from start, distance MP).

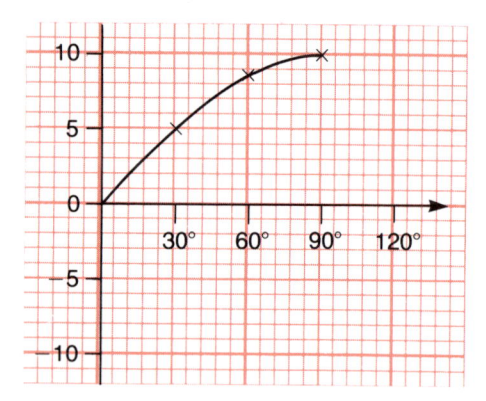

A5 Use your graph from question A4 to find the distance of the mark above or below the starting point after the wheel has turned

(a) 65° (b) 350° (c) 215°

A6 At what angles would the distance above or below the start be 5 cm?

A7 At what angles would the distance above or below the start be 7·5 cm?

A8 Write down another three angles at which the distance of the mark above or below the start would be the same as at 32°.

A9 Here is a diagram of the wheel after a turn of 50°.

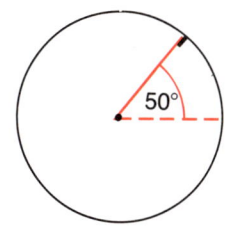

Copy the diagram and on it mark clearly the other three places at which the mark would be the same distance above or below the starting point.

A10 Explain how you can find sets of points at which the mark is the same distance above or below the starting point.

A11 What would happen on your graph from question A4 if the wheel continued turning after it had reached 360°?

A12 Draw diagrams to show the position of the mark after turns of
(a) 465° (b) 562° (c) −135° (d) −390°

B Trigonometric ratios

Diagrams like these, which show an amount of turning, are called **rotating-arm diagrams**.

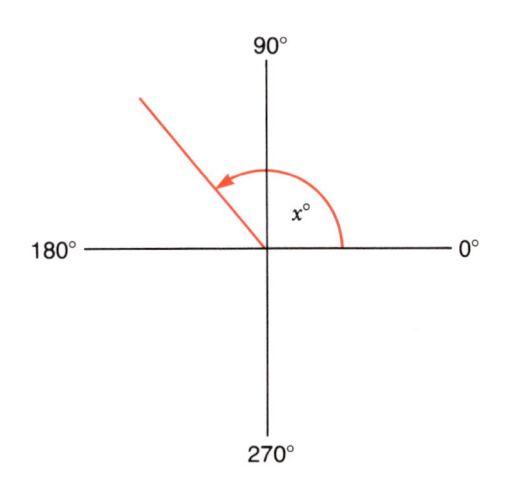

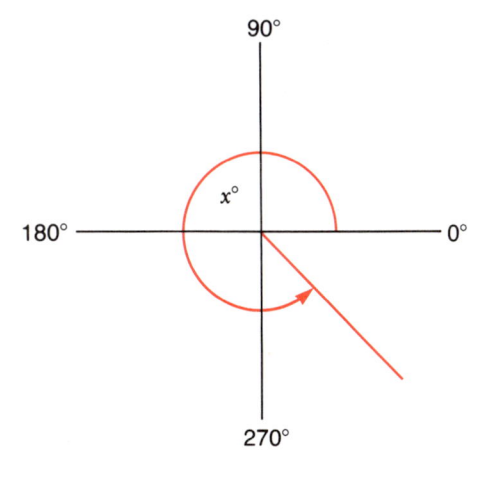

So far in trigonometry, we have dealt only with right-angled triangles with angles less than 90° in size.

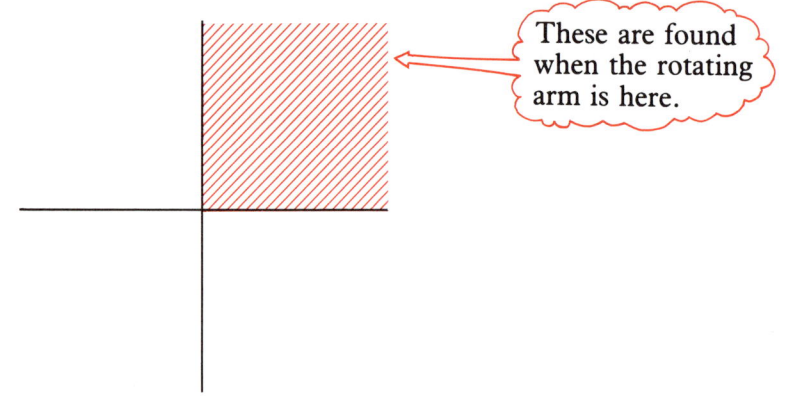

These are found when the rotating arm is here.

We must now consider what happens when the rotating arm is in *any* of the quadrants.

B1 **First quadrant**

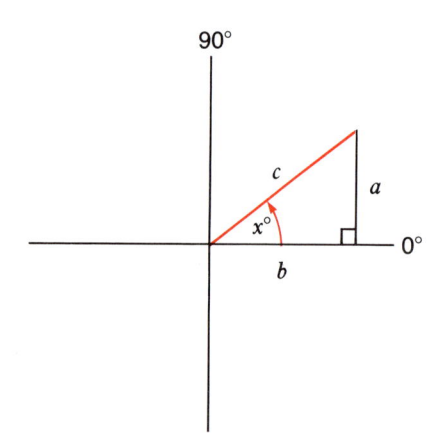

Copy the diagram.

(a) Write down the values of sin $x°$, cos $x°$ and tan $x°$.

(b) Which of these are positive? Which are negative?

B2 **Second quadrant**

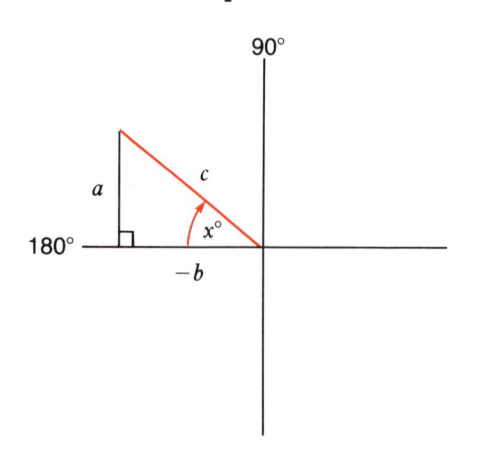

Copy the diagram.

(a) Write down the values of sin $x°$, cos $x°$ and tan $x°$.

(b) Which of these are positive? Which are negative?

B3 Third quadrant

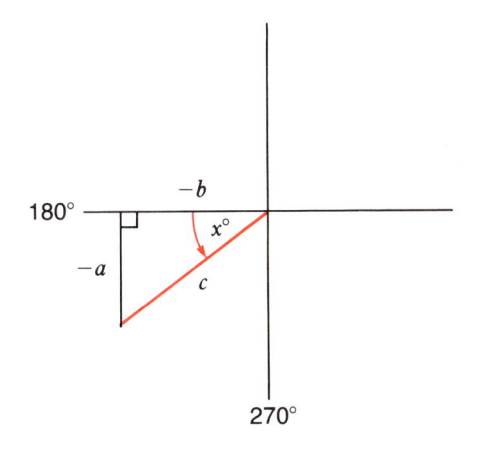

Copy the diagram.

(a) Write down the values of sin x°, cos x° and tan x°.

(b) Which of these are positive? Which are negative?

B4 Fourth quadrant

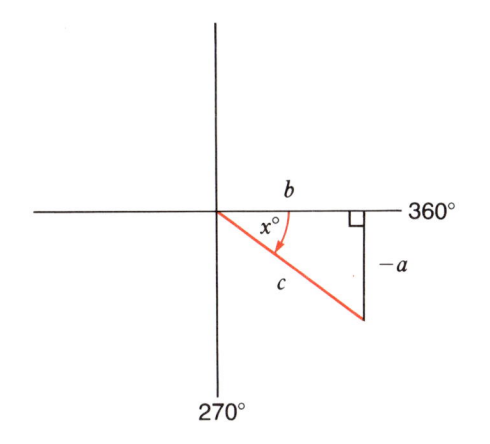

Copy the diagram.

(a) Write down the values of sin x°, cos x° and tan x°.

(b) Which of these are positive? Which are negative?

B5 Copy the diagram below.

(a) Complete the diagram by drawing the triangles for each of the other three quadrants.

(b) In each box, write the name of the function which is positive in that quadrant.

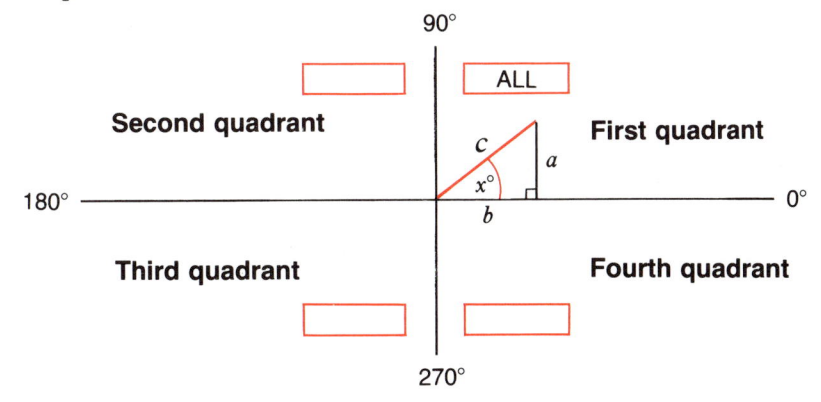

When your diagram for question B5 is complete, it should remind you of a bow tie.

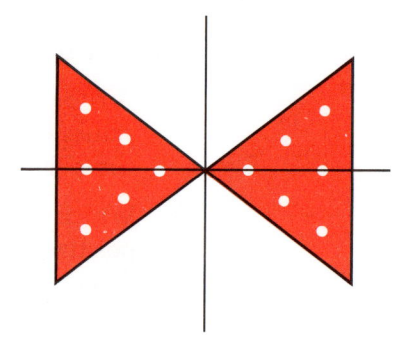

We shall use this idea in the rest of the chapter.

C Angles greater than 90°

For each of the angles given in questions C1 to C6, work out

(a) which quadrant it lies in

(b) which part of the 'bow tie' diagram applies, and draw it

(c) whether its sine, cosine and tangent are positive or negative

Parts of the first two have been done for you.

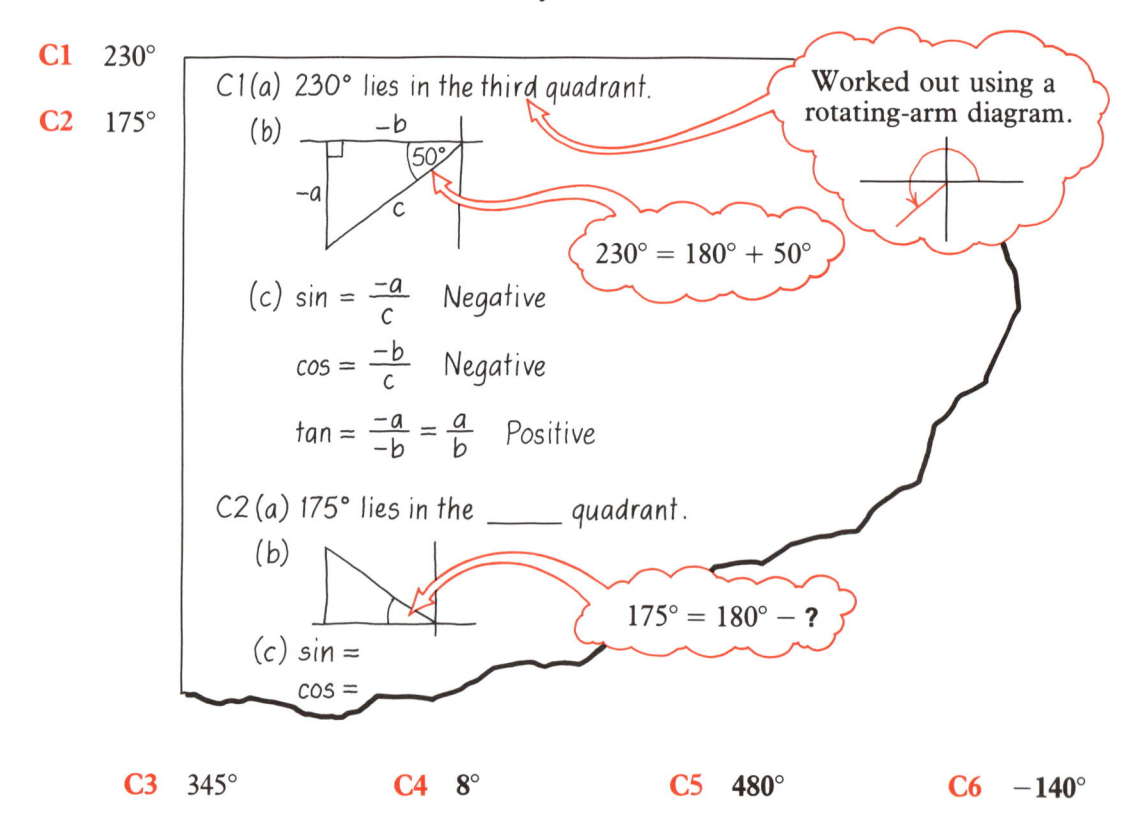

C1 230°

C2 175°

C1(a) 230° lies in the third quadrant. *Worked out using a rotating-arm diagram.*

(b) [diagram with $-b$, $-a$, c, 50°]

$230° = 180° + 50°$

(c) $\sin = \dfrac{-a}{c}$ Negative

$\cos = \dfrac{-b}{c}$ Negative

$\tan = \dfrac{-a}{-b} = \dfrac{a}{b}$ Positive

C2 (a) 175° lies in the _____ quadrant.

(b) [diagram]

$175° = 180° - ?$

(c) $\sin =$

$\cos =$

C3 345°   **C4** 8°   **C5** 480°   **C6** −140°

D Trigonometric ratios of angles greater than 90°

We can take this idea a step further and calculate the values of the sine, cosine and tangent of any angle. For example, we can calculate cos 230° like this.

1 Work out which quadrant the angle lies in.

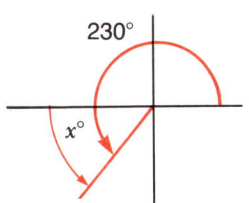

230° lies in the third quadrant.

2 Draw the correct part of the 'bow tie'.

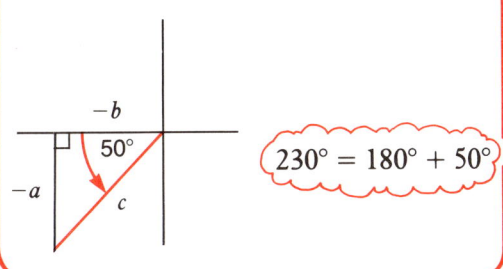

230° = 180° + 50°

3 Work out the sine, cosine or tangent of $x°$.

cos 50° = 0·643

4 Work out if the required ratio is positive or negative.

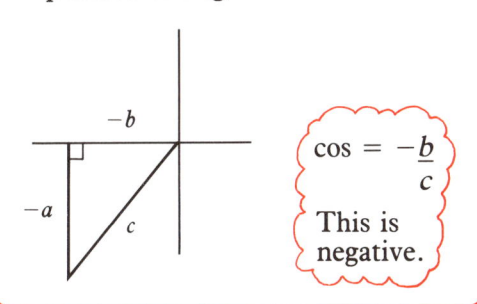

$\cos = -\dfrac{b}{c}$

This is negative.

5 Write down the answer.

cos 230° = −cos 50° = −0·643

D1 Calculate each of the following trigonometric ratios.

Part of the first one has been done for you.

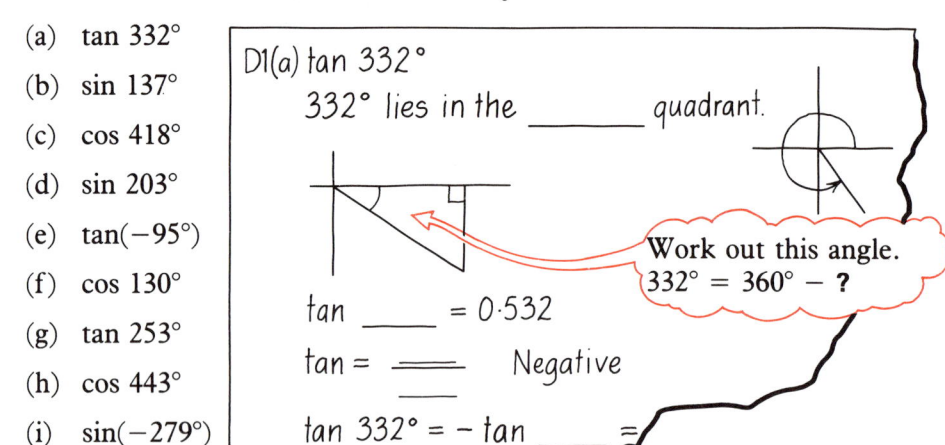

(a) tan 332°
(b) sin 137°
(c) cos 418°
(d) sin 203°
(e) tan(−95°)
(f) cos 130°
(g) tan 253°
(h) cos 443°
(i) sin(−279°)

D1(a) tan 332°

332° lies in the _____ quadrant.

Work out this angle.
332° = 360° − ?

tan _____ = 0·532

tan = $\dfrac{}{}$ Negative

tan 332° = − tan _____ =

E Special angles greater than 90°

In chapter 3, we found that the trigonometric ratios of 30°, 45° and 60° could be given as exact values, as shown in the table below.

	30°	45°	60°
sine	$\dfrac{1}{2}$	$\dfrac{1}{\sqrt{2}}$	$\dfrac{\sqrt{3}}{2}$
cosine	$\dfrac{\sqrt{3}}{2}$	$\dfrac{1}{\sqrt{2}}$	$\dfrac{1}{2}$
tangent	$\dfrac{1}{\sqrt{3}}$	1	$\sqrt{3}$

We can use this table to help work out values of the sine, cosine and tangent of larger angles involving 30°, 45° and 60°. For example, we can work out sin 120° like this.

1 120° lies in the second quadrant.

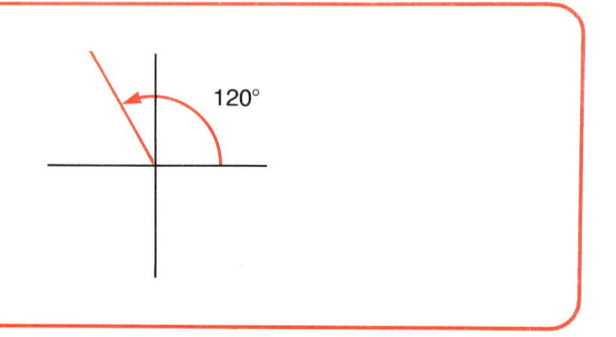

120°

2 $120° = 180° - 60°$ $\sin 60° = \dfrac{\sqrt{3}}{2}$

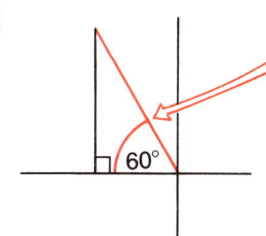

$\sin = \dfrac{a}{c}$ Positive

3 $\sin 120° = \sin 60° = \dfrac{\sqrt{3}}{2}$

E1 Work out exact values for each of these trigonometric ratios.

(a) $\cos 120°$ (b) $\tan 330°$ (c) $\sin 135°$

(d) $\cos 315°$ (e) $\tan(-225°)$ (f) $\sin 660°$

F Review

Let us take a few minutes to consider what we have been doing.

F1 Think about $\tan 160°$.

(a) What angle's tangent would you look up in your tables?
(b) Why this angle?
(c) How would you work out the *sign* of $\tan 160°$?
(d) How many angles between 0° and 360° have a tangent equal to that of 160°?

F2 Think about $\sin 135°$.

(a) What angle's sine would you look up in your tables?
(b) Why this angle?
(c) How would you work out the *sign* of $\sin 135°$?
(d) How many angles between 0° and 360° have a sine equal to that of 135°?

F3 Here is a puzzle: $\cos ?° = 0·342$

(a) How many possible answers are there for this puzzle, if you are told that the angle lies between 0° and 360°?

(b) In which quadrants do they lie?

(c) If the angle can be any size, which of the following are possible solutions?

70° 140° 250° 290° 430° 470° 610° 650° 1510° 2270°

Give reasons for your answers.

F4 Try to find two solutions for each of the following puzzles, if the angle lies between 0° and 360°.

(a) $\sin ? = 0·643$

(b) $\tan ? = -11·43$

(c) $\cos ? = -0·883$

(d) $\cos ? = \dfrac{1}{\sqrt{2}}$

(e) $\tan ? = -\sqrt{3}$

G Trigonometric equations

The puzzles you were solving in section F are really equations. We call them **trigonometric equations**, since they involve sines, cosines and tangents.

Worked example

Calculate the value of y if $\cos y° = -0·235$.

1 Work out which parts of the 'bow tie' diagram apply.

Cosine is negative: or

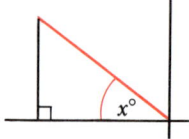

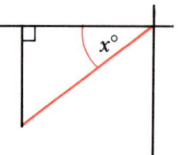

Angle is in the second or third quadrant.

2 Work out the angle $x°$.

Acute angle whose cosine is 0·235 is 76·4°.

3 Work out the necessary values.

Second quadrant: $180° - 76·4° = 103·6°$
Third quadrant: $180° + 76·4° = 256·4°$

4 Write down the answer. $y = 103 \cdot 6$ or $y = 256 \cdot 4$

G1 Calculate the possible sizes of each of these unknown angles.
(a) $\sin a° = 0 \cdot 736$
(b) $\tan b° = -3 \cdot 2$
(c) $\cos c° = -0 \cdot 539$
(d) $\sin d° = -0 \cdot 201$
(e) $\cos e° = -2 \cdot 0$
(f) $\tan f° = -3 \cdot 0$

Here is a harder trigonometric equation.

This is like

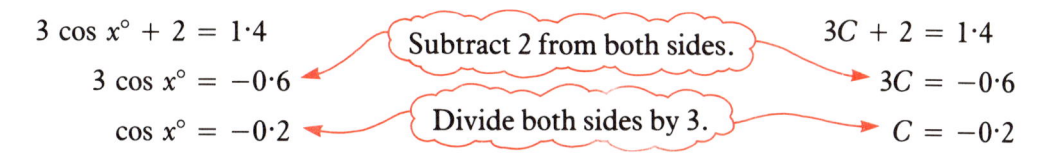

$3 \cos x° + 2 = 1 \cdot 4$ Subtract 2 from both sides. $3C + 2 = 1 \cdot 4$
$3 \cos x° = -0 \cdot 6$ $3C = -0 \cdot 6$
$\cos x° = -0 \cdot 2$ Divide both sides by 3. $C = -0 \cdot 2$

We can take the trigonometric equation one step further.

The cosine is negative, so $x°$ lies in the second or third quadrant.

The acute angle is $78 \cdot 5°$.

Second quadrant: $180° - 78 \cdot 5° = 101 \cdot 5°$
Third quadrant: $180° + 78 \cdot 5° = 258 \cdot 5°$

So $x = 101 \cdot 5$ or $x = 258 \cdot 5$.

G2 Calculate possible sizes for $x°$ in each of these equations, if $x°$ lies between $0°$ and $360°$.
(a) $4 \tan x° - 5 = 0$
(b) $3 \sin x° + 4 = 2 \cdot 4$
(c) $5 - \cos x° = 4$
(d) $7 - 3 \tan x° = 2 \cdot 9$
(e) $\frac{1}{2} \sin x° + 2 = 3$

H Identities

In chapter 3, we investigated the following results.

$\sin^2 x° + \cos^2 x° = 1$

$\frac{\sin x°}{\cos x°} = \tan x°$

$\sin x° = \cos(90° - x°)$

$\cos x° = \sin(90° - x°)$

We shall now try to see if these results hold for some other angles, starting with 334°.

1 Work out the sine, cosine and tangent.

$\sin 334° = -0·438$
$\cos 334° = 0·899$
$\tan 334° = -0·488$

2 Try out each rule in turn.

$\sin^2 x° + \cos^2 x° = 1?$

$\sin^2 x° + \cos^2 x°$
$= (-0·438)^2 + (0·899)^2$
$= 0·192 + 0·808$
$= 1$

Does it work?   YES

$\dfrac{\sin x°}{\cos x°} = \tan x°?$

$\dfrac{\sin x°}{\cos x°} = \dfrac{-0·438}{0·899}$

$= -0·487$

Does it work?   ALMOST

$\sin x° = \cos(90° - x°)?$

$90° - 334° = -244°$
$\cos(-244°) = -0·438$

Does it work?   YES

$\cos x° = \sin(90° - x°)?$

$\sin(-244)° = 0·899$

Does it work?   YES

H1 Can you explain why $\dfrac{\sin x°}{\cos x°}$ is only *almost* equal to tan x°?

H2 How could you ensure that this did not happen?

H3 Check that the rules hold for each of the following angles.

(a) 120°   (b) 225°   (c) 432°   (d) −35°   (e) 753°

Use a scientific calculator to help you, if you have one.

H4 Check that the rules hold for two angles of your own choice.

Since these rules hold for every angle, they are called **identities**. Both sides of the equation are identical in value.

H5 Investigation

Try to work out an identity which links $\dfrac{1}{\cos x°}$ and tan x°.

(**Hint:** Try squaring them.)

I The algebra of identities

Sometimes, we are asked to prove that a statement is an identity. To do this, we start with one side of the equation and show that it is identical in value to the other side, using all the algebraic processes we have learnt.

Worked example

Prove that $3 \sin^2 x° + 3 \sin^2(90° - x°) = 3$

$$\begin{aligned}\text{Left-hand side} &= 3 \sin^2 x° + 3 \sin^2(90° - x°) \\ &= 3(\sin^2 x° + \sin^2(90° - x°)) \\ &= 3(\sin^2 x° + \cos^2 x°) \\ &= 3 \times 1 \\ &= 3 \\ &= \text{Right-hand side}\end{aligned}$$

Common factor

$\sin(90° - x°) = \cos x°$
so $\sin^2(90° - x°) = \cos^2 x°$

so $3 \sin^2 x° + 3 \sin^2(90° - x°) = 3$

I1 Prove that each of the following equations is an identity.

(a) $5 \sin^2 x° + 5 \cos^2 x° = 5$

(b) $\dfrac{2 \sin x°}{4 \cos x°} = \tfrac{1}{2} \tan x°$

(c) $6 \cos^2 A° = 6 - 6 \sin^2 A°$

(d) $(\cos A° + \sin A°)^2 = 1 + 2 \sin A° \cos A°$

(e) $(\sin(90° - a°) + \cos a°)^2 = 4 \cos^2 a°$

(f) $\dfrac{\sin A°}{\cos A°} + \dfrac{\cos A°}{\sin A°} = \dfrac{1}{\cos A° \sin A°}$

Money management 4: savings and investment

A Interest

Both Cathy and Colin know that it is important to save money regularly. Cathy has been looking at various ways that they can do this, so that they get the best return on their money. The schemes she has looked at fall into three main categories. We shall look at each of these in turn, and see what happens to £100 invested for five years in each type of scheme.

1 No interest

Under this type of scheme, the amount of money remains the same, no matter how long it has been invested. Some examples include some bank 'current accounts' and savings stamps – as well as keeping money in an old sock or under the mattress! These schemes are best suited for saving money which will be used quickly.

Example

£100 is invested for five years in a current account at a bank.

The amount in the bank after five years is still £100.

2 Simple interest

Under this type of scheme, a given percentage of the original amount invested is added on for every year the money remains in the bank. This extra money is called **interest**. The total interest is the interest for one year multiplied by the number of years the money is invested. If the money is invested for less than one year, this number will be a fraction (for example, it will be $\frac{1}{2}$ if the money is invested for six months).

Example

£100 is invested for five years in an account at the Bank of Moremoney which offers 6% simple interest.

$$\text{Interest} = £100 \times 6\% \times 5$$
$$= £30$$

- Amount invested
- Number of years the money is invested
- Annual rate of interest

The amount in the bank after five years is £130.

3 Compound interest

Under this type of scheme, the interest is added onto the money in the account after a given period (usually one month, six months or one year). The interest for the next period is calculated as a percentage of this new amount, and so on.

Example

£100 is invested for five years in an account at the Bank of Yetmoremoney which offers 6% compound interest.

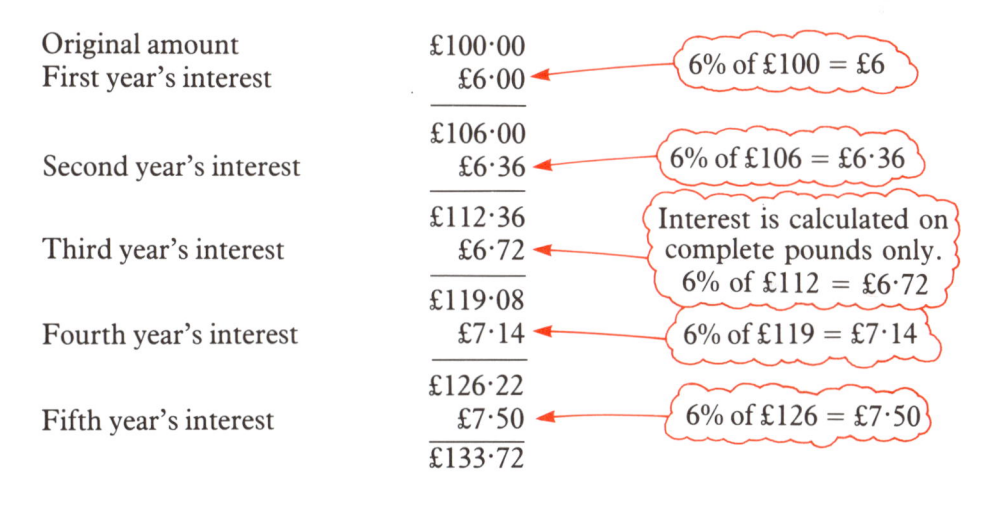

Original amount	£100·00	
First year's interest	£6·00	6% of £100 = £6
	£106·00	
Second year's interest	£6·36	6% of £106 = £6·36
	£112·36	Interest is calculated on complete pounds only.
Third year's interest	£6·72	6% of £112 = £6·72
	£119·08	
Fourth year's interest	£7·14	6% of £119 = £7·14
	£126·22	
Fifth year's interest	£7·50	6% of £126 = £7·50
	£133·72	

The amount in the bank after five years is £133·72.

This is the best of the three types of interest for amounts of money invested for longer than a year.

A1 Calculate how much money would be in the bank at the end of each of the following investments.

(a) £300 invested for two years with simple interest at a rate of 7% per annum.

(b) £250 invested for five years with simple interest at a rate of 9·5% per annum.

(c) £400 invested for six months with simple interest at a rate of 7·65% per annum.

(d) £175 invested for seven months with simple interest at a rate of x% per annum.

(e) £50 invested for three years with an interest rate of 5%, compounded annually.

(f) £300 invested for four years with an interest rate of 11·13%, compounded annually.

(g) £250 invested for two years with an interest rate of 10·05%, compounded six-monthly. (10·05% interest is added every six months.)

A2 John invests £200 for one year in a scheme which offers simple interest. At the end of the year he has £216 in the bank.

Calculate the annual rate of interest.

A3 Susan invested £325 for six months in a simple interest scheme and received £5 interest at the end of the period.

Calculate the annual rate of interest.

A4 Robert wants to earn £500 interest from his money each year. His bank offers simple interest at a rate of 5% per annum.

How much money would Robert have to invest?

A5 Julie invested £225 in a scheme with simple interest at a rate of 12% per annum. At the end of the period, she had £393·75 in the bank.

For how long (to the nearest month) did Julie invest her money?

B Investigation

Cathy and Colin ask the people at Flash Cash to advise them on the savings schemes that would best suit their needs. Cathy tells them

Colin and I are engaged to be married and we want to save at least £2000 over the next two years. I can afford to save £35 per month. Colin can afford to save £10 per week.

Here are her notes on the schemes that Flash Cash suggest.

> Bank Special Investment Account:
> 9% interest compounded six-monthly
> Amounts over £500 only
> Must give 3 months' notice of any withdrawal
>
> Building Society Ordinary Account:
> 7% interest compounded six-monthly
>
> National Savings Investment Account:
> 9½% interest compounded six-monthly
> Amounts over £1000 only
>
> Monthly Savings Account in Building Society:
> 8% interest compounded six-monthly
> Must save set amount each month
> Only allowed one withdrawal per year

B1 Plan a combination of schemes that will give Cathy and Colin a good return on their money and which you think best suits their needs. Give reasons for your choices.

(It is possible to save money in one account and then transfer it to another.)

C Stocks and shares

Another way of investing money is in **stocks** and **shares**. These are bought and sold on the Stock Exchange. Shares are small parts of a company; stocks are a loan to a large company or to the government.

If you buy stock, you are paid interest at a fixed rate, for example, $4\frac{1}{2}$% War Stock would give an annual rate of interest of $4\frac{1}{2}$%.

Worked example

Robert invested £3000 in $3\frac{1}{4}$% War Stock for four years. Calculate the interest due at the end of this period.

Interest per year   = $3\frac{1}{4}$% of £3000 = £97·50
Interest after four years = 4 × £97·50 = £390

The interest you receive from shares (called the **dividend**) depends on how well the company is doing.

Before investing in shares, investors should calculate how much they expect to get back from the money they are going to invest. This is called the **yield**, and it is usually given as a percentage.

Worked example

Mary bought 200 shares in Roots at 221p each.
Calculate her expected dividend if the yield was 5%.

Yield per share = 5% of 221p = 11·05p
Total dividend = 200 × 11·05 = £22·10

Here are some examples for you to try.

C1 Emma invested £1250 in 6½% Loan Stock for two years.

Work out the interest due to her at the end of this period.

C2 Alan invested £7500 in 3¼% War Stock in 1939.

How much interest would he be due in 1999?

C3 Calculate the expected dividends if £500 is invested in the shares of each of these companies.

Company	Cost per share	Yield
Tesbury's	160p	2·2%
Overwood's	204p	3%
Cowntree	399p	4·9%

6 Similar triangles

In the book *Scouting for Boys*, which was written by Lord Baden-Powell in 1908, there is a method for finding the height of an object such as a tree.

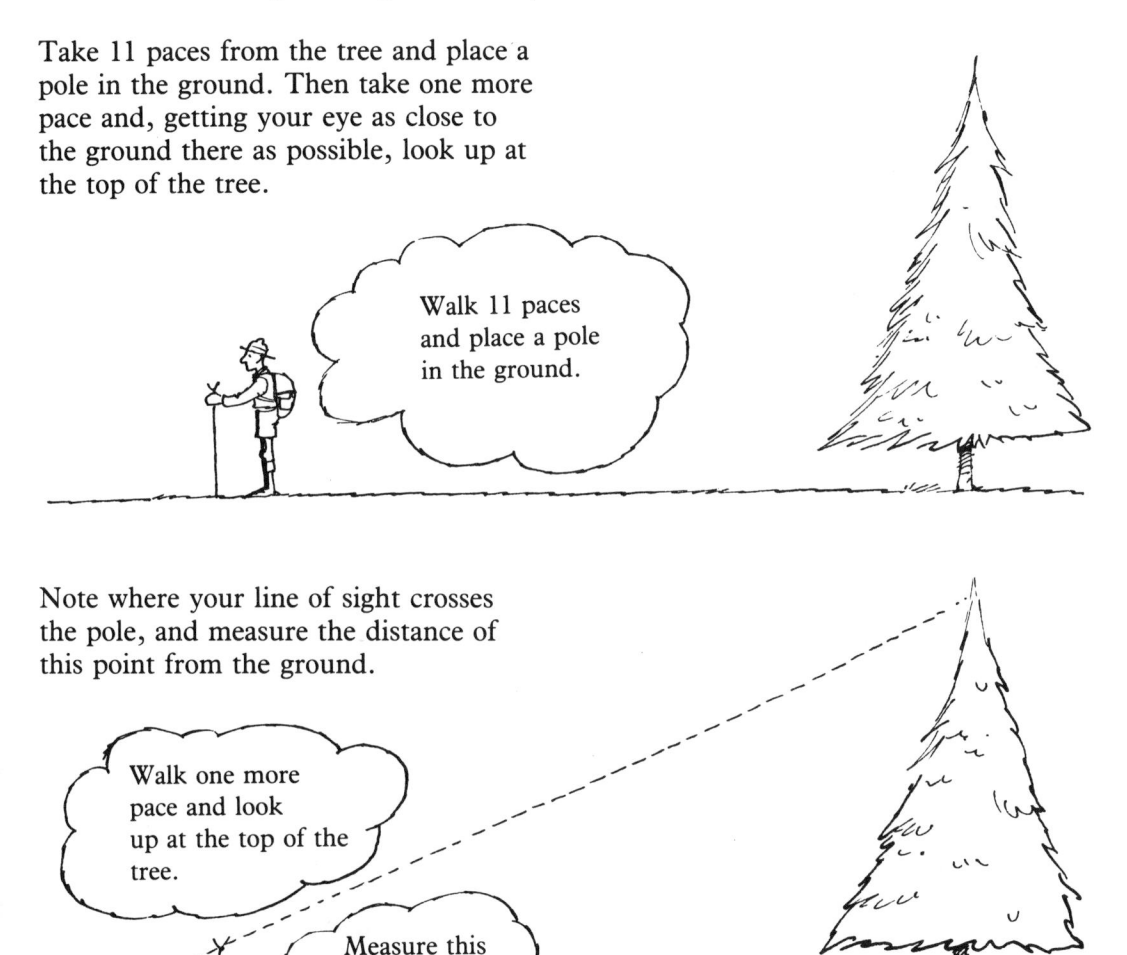

Take 11 paces from the tree and place a pole in the ground. Then take one more pace and, getting your eye as close to the ground there as possible, look up at the top of the tree.

> Walk 11 paces and place a pole in the ground.

Note where your line of sight crosses the pole, and measure the distance of this point from the ground.

> Walk one more pace and look up at the top of the tree.

> Measure this distance.

To calculate the height of the tree, multiply the distance measured by 12.

This is a tried and tested method – but how does it work?

It uses the idea of 'similar triangles', which we will study in this chapter.

A Equiangular triangles

Look at these two triangles.

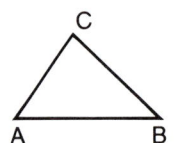

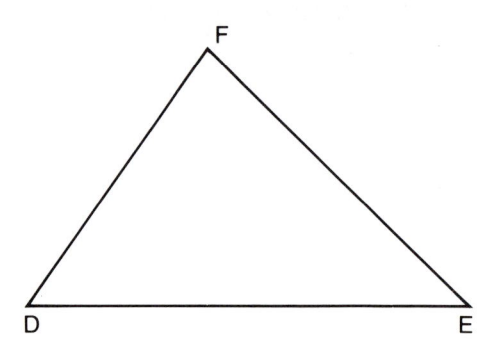

Triangle DEF is an enlargement of triangle ABC.

A1 Copy and complete this table.

Triangle ABC	Triangle DEF
AB = BC = AC =	DE = EF = DF =

A2 What is the scale factor of the enlargement?

A3 How do you know this?

A4 Now add two more columns to your table from question A1.

Measure the angles of both triangles using a protractor and fill in the extra two columns.

Triangle ABC	Triangle DEF
$\hat{A}$ = $\hat{B}$ = $\hat{C}$ =	$\hat{D}$ = $\hat{E}$ = $\hat{H}$ =

A5 What do you notice about the angles of the triangles?

A6 Using squared paper, draw an obtuse-angled triangle ABC and an enlargement or reduction of it labelled DEF.

A7 Make a table like the one in question A4 and complete the four columns as before.

If we have an enlargement or a reduction of a triangle, the angles in the two triangles are equal, and the triangles are said to be *equiangular* ('equi' means 'equal').

A8 In these pairs of triangles, one triangle is an enlargement or reduction of the other.

Find the sizes of the unlabelled angles.

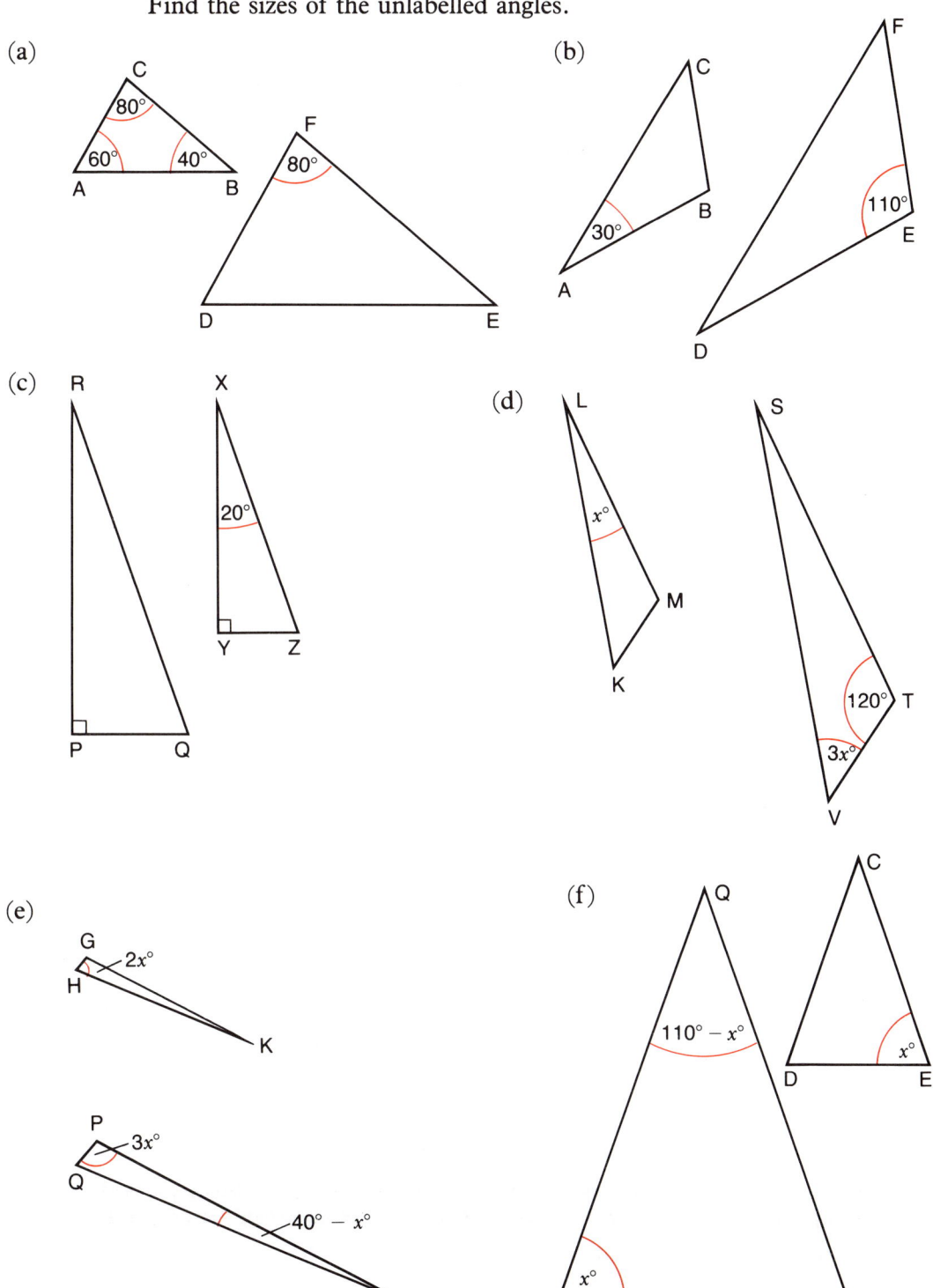

(a)

(b)

(c)

(d)

(e)

(f)

85

B Corresponding sides

Look at these two equiangular triangles.

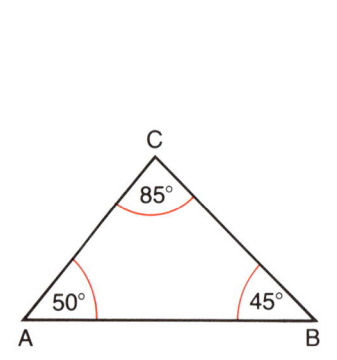

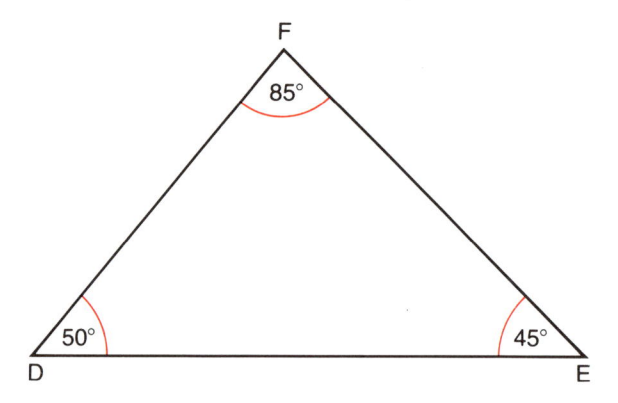

B1 Copy and complete this table.

Triangle ABC	Triangle DEF	Ratio
AB =	DE =	$\dfrac{AB}{DE} =$
BC =	EF =	$\dfrac{BC}{EF} =$
AC =	DF =	$\dfrac{AC}{DF} =$

B2 Copy and complete this sentence.

In two equiangular triangles, the ratios of the sides opposite the equal angles . . .

B3 Construct two equiangular triangles with angles of 35°, 65° and 80°. Label them ABC and DEF.

B4 Make a table like the one in question B1 and, by measuring the sides of your triangles, fill in the three columns. (You may need to use a calculator for the 'ratio' column – round your answers to two significant figures.)

B5 Repeat questions B3 and B4 for another pair of equiangular triangles with angles of your own choice.

If we have two equiangular triangles, then the ratios of the three pairs of corresponding sides are all the same. ('Corresponding sides' means sides in the same position in both triangles – they are always opposite equal angles.)

B6 Make tables to show the corresponding sides in each of these pairs of equiangular triangles. Make a different table for each pair of triangles. The first one has been started for you.

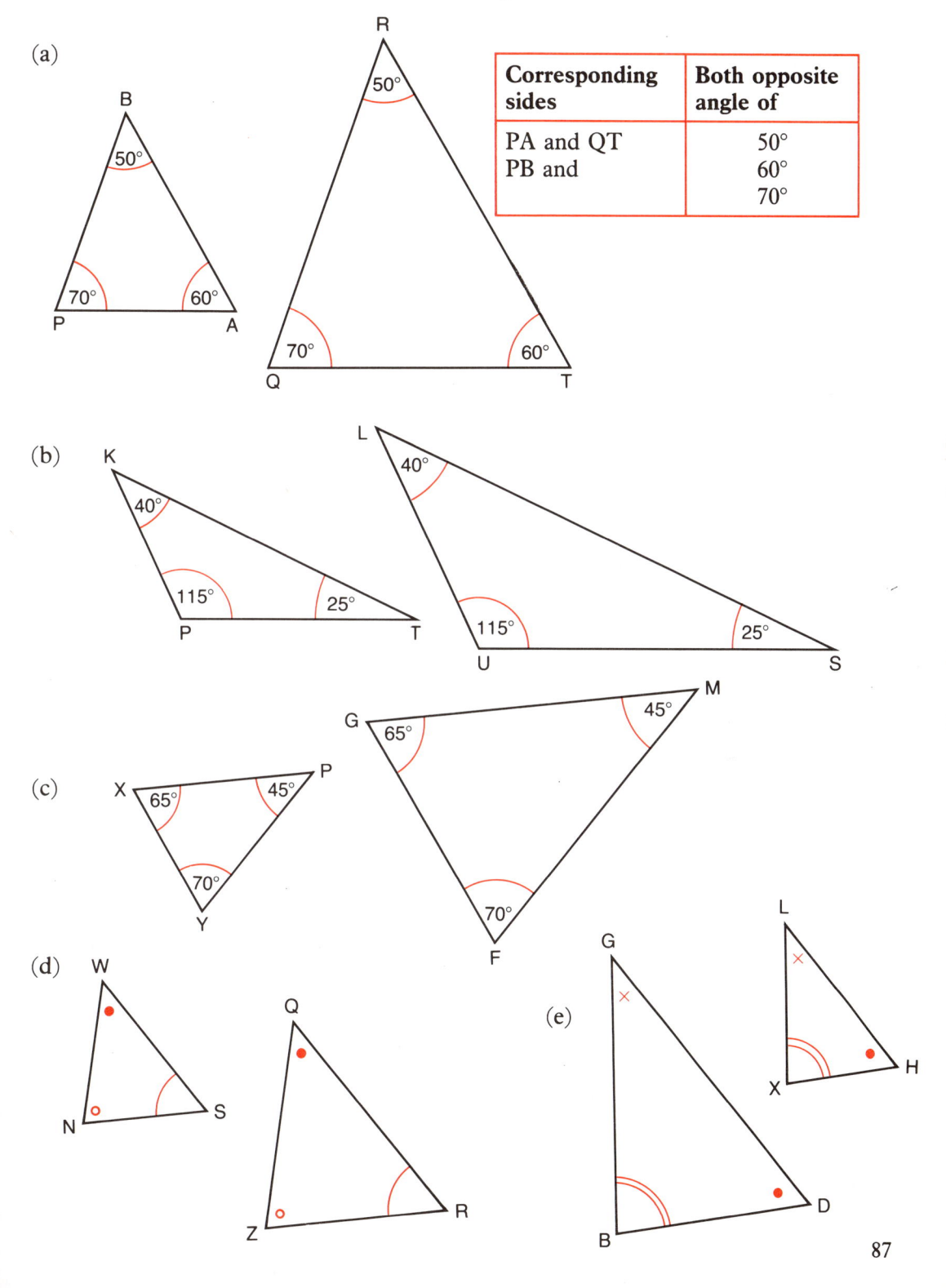

(a)

Corresponding sides	Both opposite angle of
PA and QT PB and	50° 60° 70°

(b)

(c)

(d)

(e)

C Using similar triangles to show that angles are equal

From sections A and B we now know

(1) If the ratios of corresponding sides in two triangles are all equal, then the triangles are equiangular.

(2) If two triangles are equiangular, then the ratios of their corresponding sides are all equal.

Any shapes (not just triangles) which are equiangular *and* have the ratios of their corresponding sides equal are said to be **similar**.

Triangles are a special case. To prove that two triangles are similar, it is sufficient to prove that they are equiangular *or* that the ratios of their corresponding sides are equal.

Worked example

Are these two triangles similar? If they are, which angles are equal?

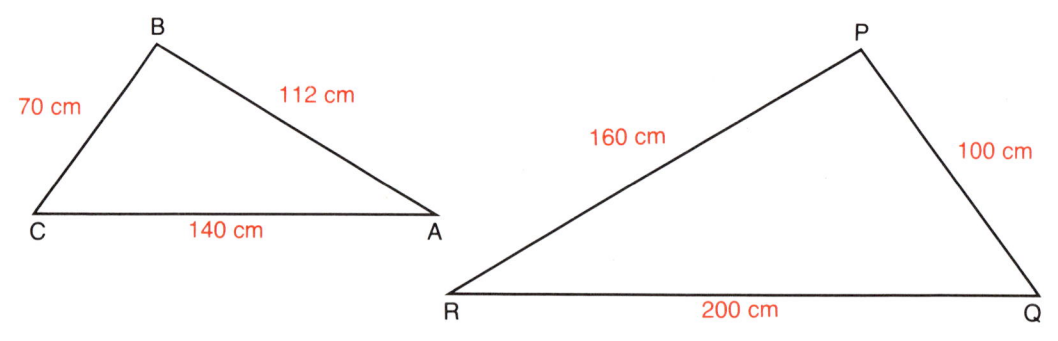

If all three ratios are to be the same, then the two longest sides must be corresponding sides, so must the two shortest sides, and so must the two middle sides.

$$\text{Ratio of the two longest sides} = \frac{140}{200} = \frac{7}{10}$$

$$\text{Ratio of the two shortest sides} = \frac{70}{100} = \frac{7}{10}$$

$$\text{Ratio of the two middle sides} = \frac{112}{160} = \frac{7}{10}$$

Since all three ratios are the same, the triangles are similar and are therefore equiangular.

The two longest sides, AC and RQ, are corresponding sides, so the angles opposite them are equal.

So $\hat{B} = \hat{P}$

Since the two middle sides, AB and RP, are also corresponding sides,

$\hat{C} = \hat{Q}$

This means that $\hat{A} = \hat{R}$.

C1 Give **two** reasons why $\hat{A} = \hat{R}$.

C2 By considering the ratios of sides, decide whether each of these pairs of triangles are similar. If they are, name the equal angles.

(a)

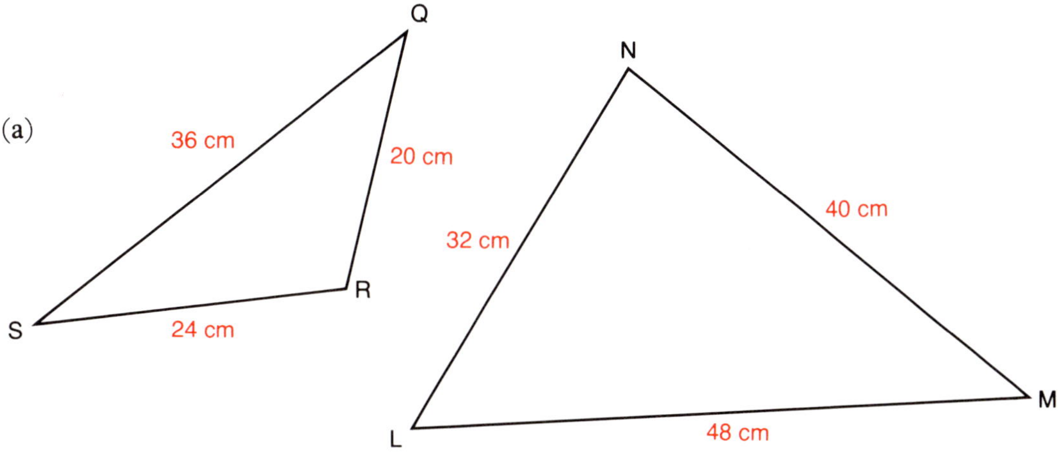

(b)

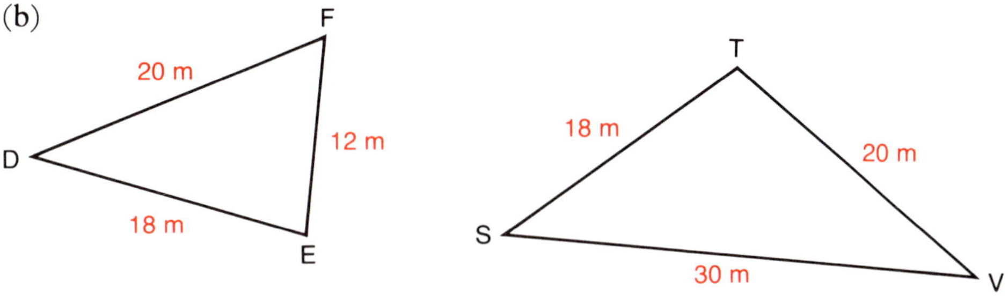

(c)

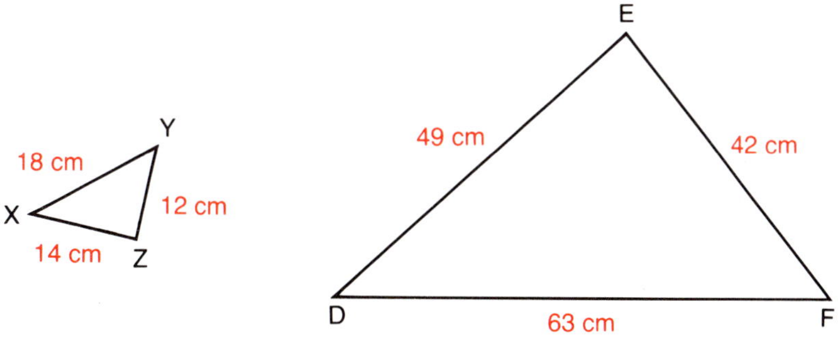

(d)

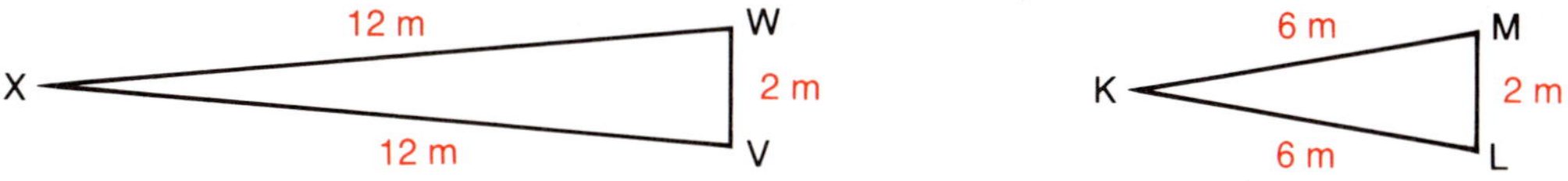

D Using similar triangles to calculate sides

Worked example

Prove that these triangles are similar, and hence calculate the length of BC.

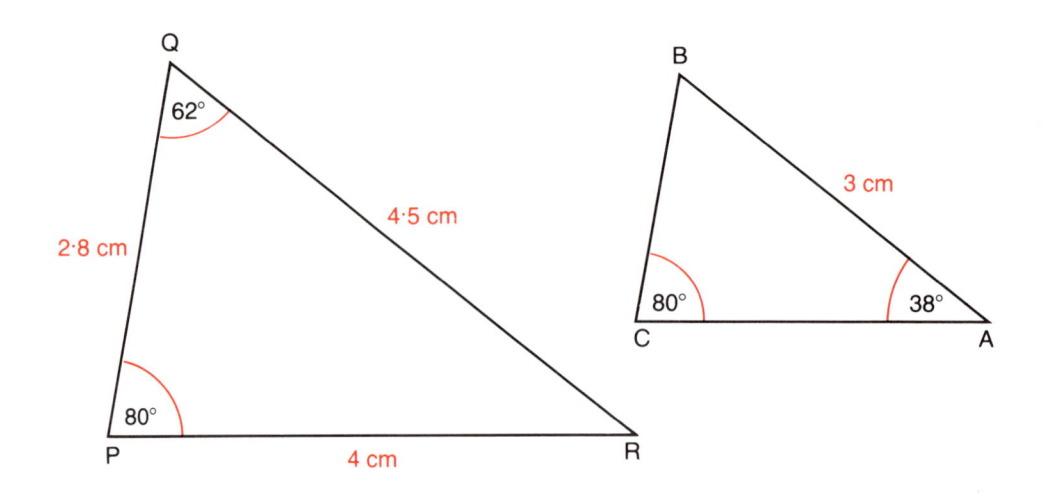

1 Prove that the triangles are similar.

In triangles PQR and ABC,

$\hat{P} = \hat{C}$ (both 80°)
$\hat{Q} = \hat{B}$ (both 62°)
$\hat{S} = \hat{A}$ (both 38°)

The triangles are equiangular.
Therefore they are similar.

Use the 80° and 38° to calculate the size of $\hat{B}$.
$\hat{B} = 180° - (80° + 38°)$

Do the same with 80° and 62° to calculate the size of $\hat{R}$.

2 Write down the ratios of the corresponding sides.

$$\frac{PR}{CA} = \frac{RQ}{AB} = \frac{QP}{BC}$$

Opposite 62° angle   *Opposite 80° angle*   *Opposite 38° angle*

Remember that corresponding sides are opposite equal angles.

3 Use the equal ratios to calculate the required side.

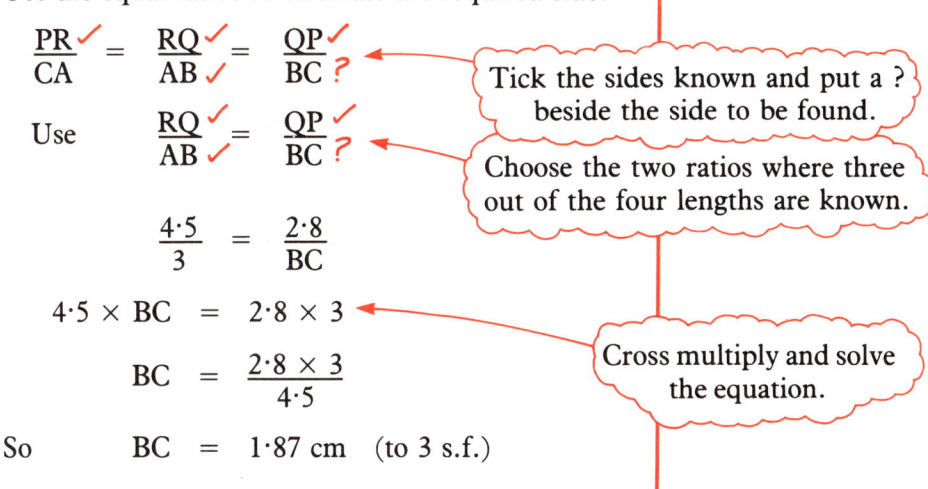

$$\frac{PR\checkmark}{CA} = \frac{RQ\checkmark}{AB\checkmark} = \frac{QP\checkmark}{BC\ ?}$$

Tick the sides known and put a ? beside the side to be found.

Use $\quad \frac{RQ\checkmark}{AB\checkmark} = \frac{QP\checkmark}{BC\ ?}$

Choose the two ratios where three out of the four lengths are known.

$$\frac{4\cdot 5}{3} = \frac{2\cdot 8}{BC}$$

$$4\cdot 5 \times BC = 2\cdot 8 \times 3$$

$$BC = \frac{2\cdot 8 \times 3}{4\cdot 5}$$

Cross multiply and solve the equation.

So $\quad BC = 1\cdot 87$ cm (to 3 s.f.)

D1 Prove that these triangles are similar, and calculate RP.

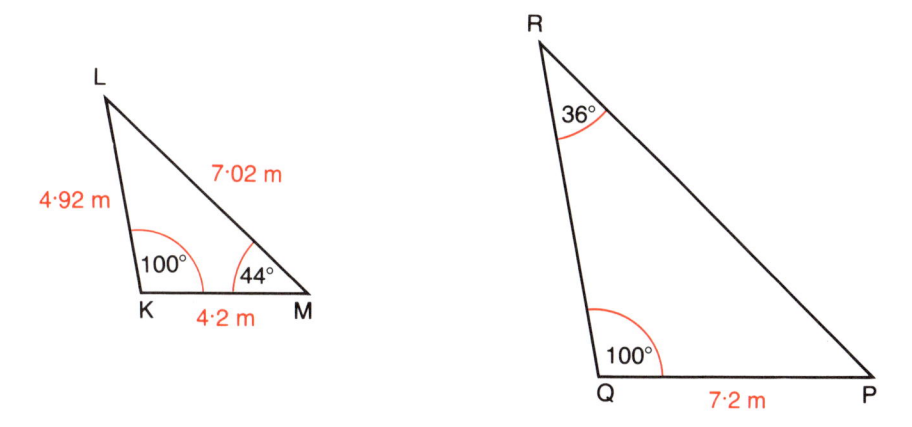

Triangle LKM: LK = 4·92 m, LM = 7·02 m, KM = 4·2 m, angle K = 100°, angle M = 44°.

Triangle RQP: angle R = 36°, angle Q = 100°, QP = 7·2 m.

D2 Prove that these triangles are similar, and calculate YZ.

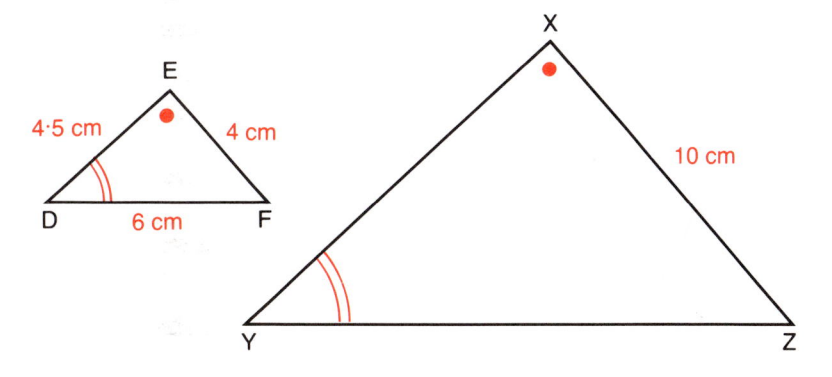

Triangle DEF: DE = 4·5 cm, EF = 4 cm, DF = 6 cm.

Triangle XYZ: XZ = 10 cm.

D3 In the diagram below, ST is parallel to RQ. Prove that triangles PQR and PTS are similar. Hence calculate QR.

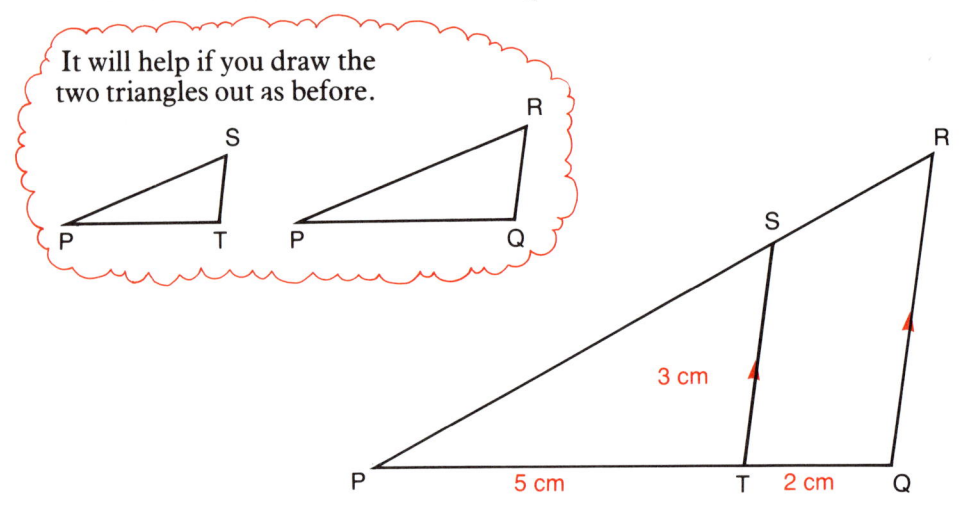

It will help if you draw the two triangles out as before.

Worked example

Prove that triangles ABC and CDE are similar. Hence calculate BC.

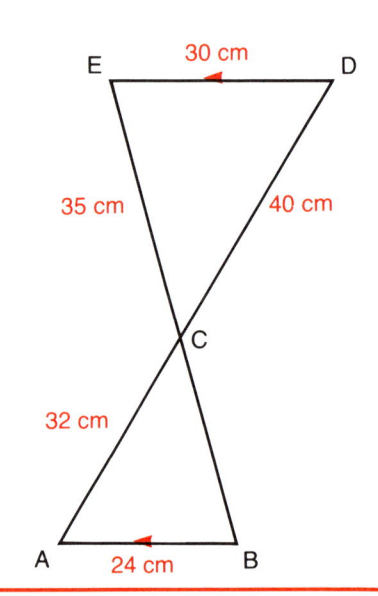

1 Mark the angles that are equal, and prove that the triangles are similar.

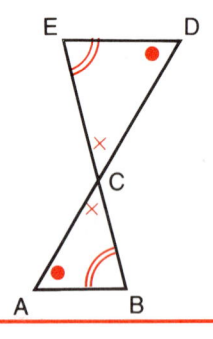

In triangles ABC and DEC,

$A\hat{B}C = C\hat{E}D$ (alternate angles)
$B\hat{A}C = C\hat{D}E$ (alternate angles)
$A\hat{C}B = E\hat{C}D$ (vertically opposite angles)

The triangles are equiangular.
Therefore they are similar.

Use three letters for each angle, as there is more than one angle at C.

*Alternate angles are marked ● and ∥
Vertically opposite angles are marked ×*

2 Sketch the triangles lying the same way round, and mark in their lengths.

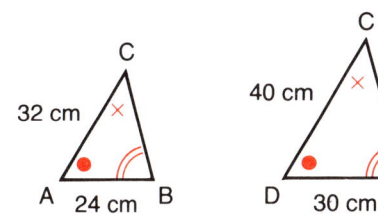

Triangle CDE has been turned round so that the angles are in the same position in both triangles.

3 Proceed as before.

$$\frac{AB\checkmark}{DE\checkmark} = \frac{BC?}{EC\checkmark} = \frac{CA\checkmark}{CD\checkmark}$$

Ratios of corresponding sides are equal.

$$\frac{BC?}{EC\checkmark} = \frac{CA\checkmark}{CD\checkmark}$$

$$\frac{BC}{35} = \frac{32}{40}$$

$$40 \times BC = 32 \times 35$$

$$BC = \frac{32 \times 35}{40}$$

$$BC = 28 \text{ cm}$$

We could also have used
$$\frac{AB\checkmark}{DE\checkmark} = \frac{BC?}{EC\checkmark}$$

D4 Prove that each of the following pairs of triangles is similar, and calculate the lengths of the sides indicated.

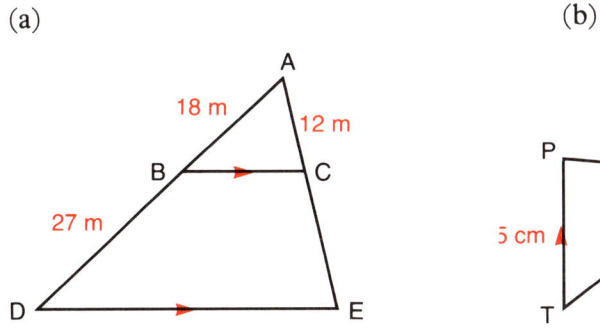

(a) Triangles ABC and ADE. Calculate AE.

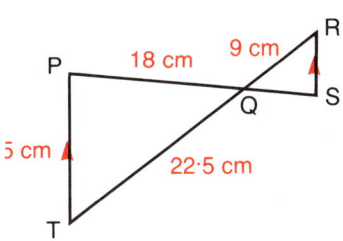

(b) Triangles PQT and QRS. Calculate RS.

(c)

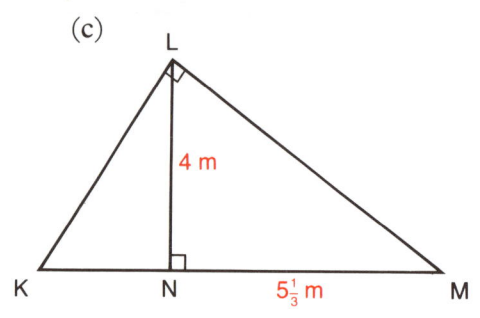

Triangles KLM and NLM.
Calculate KL.

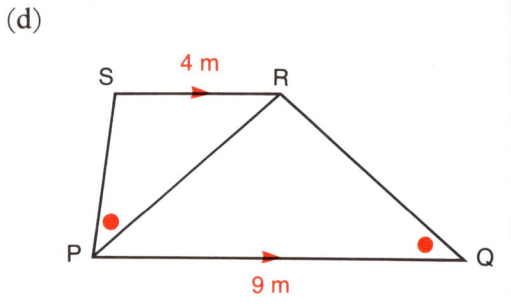

(d)

Triangles PSR and PRQ.
Calculate PR.

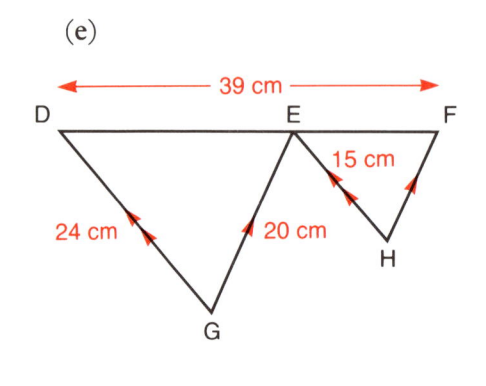

(e)

Triangles DEG and EHF.
Calculate EF.

(**Hint:** Let EF = x cm.)

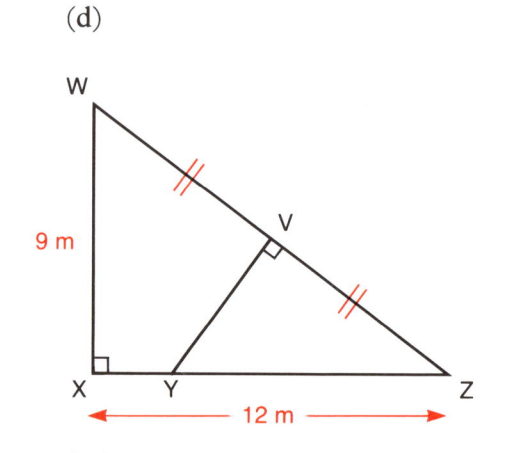

(d)

Triangles WXZ and VYZ.
Calculate VY.

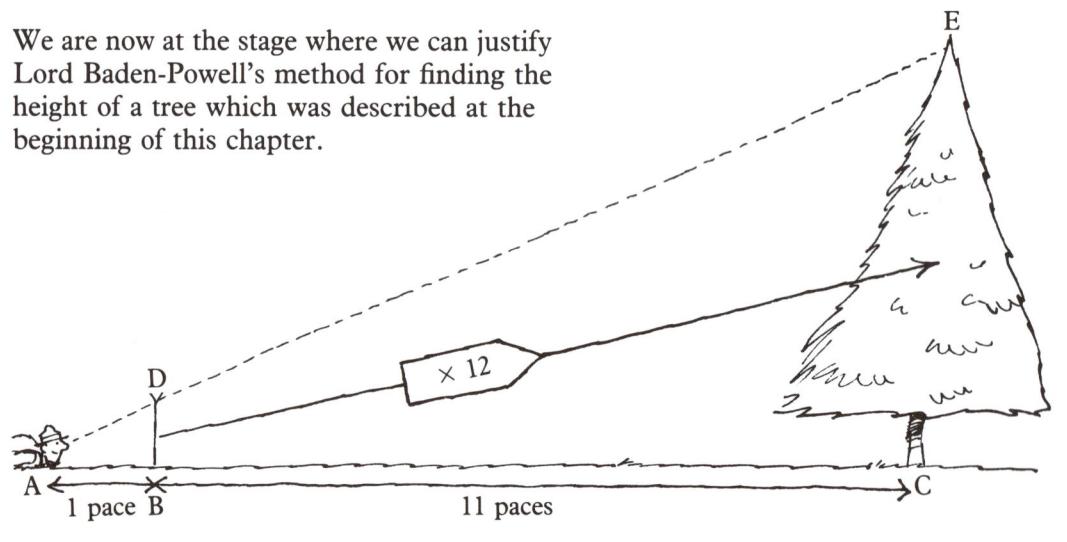

We are now at the stage where we can justify Lord Baden-Powell's method for finding the height of a tree which was described at the beginning of this chapter.

Taking the two triangles out of the diagram and marking equal angles, we get

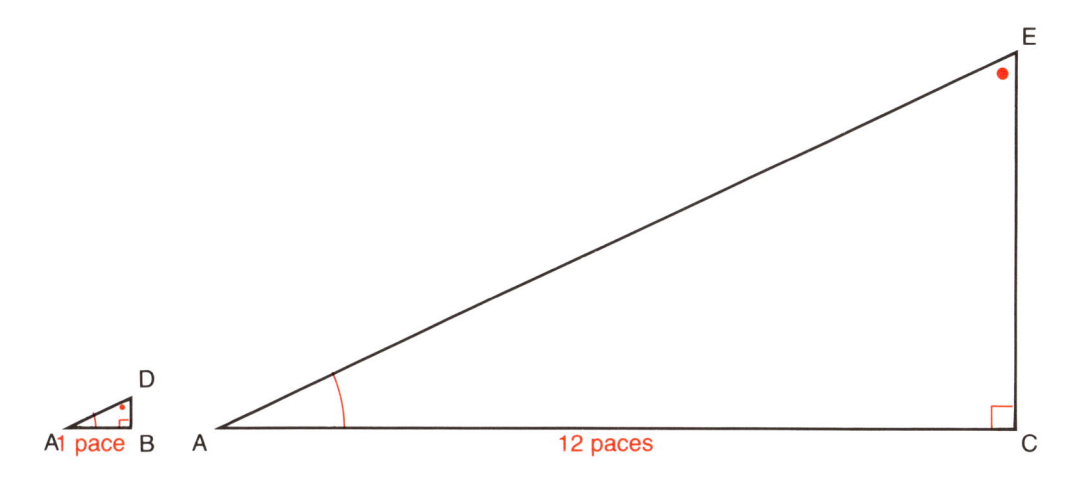

The triangles are equiangular, and therefore similar.

The ratios of the corresponding sides are

$$\frac{AD}{AE} = \frac{AB}{AC} = \frac{BD}{CE}$$

Using $\quad \dfrac{AB}{AC} = \dfrac{BD}{CE}$

$\dfrac{1}{12} = \dfrac{BD}{CE}$

and so $\quad CE = 12 \times BD$

So the height of the tree is 12 times the distance marked on the pole.

E Using similar triangles to solve real problems

A chest of drawers is to be fitted under a flight of stairs as shown in the diagram.

If the height of the chest is 1·2 m and its width is 1·8 m, will it fit in?

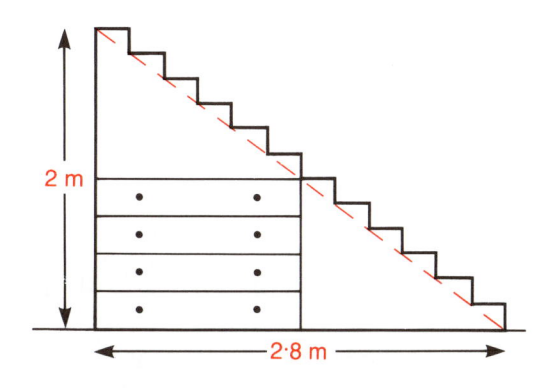

1 Draw a diagram and identify the problem.

We shall let the width of the chest of drawers be 1·8 m and calculate the maximum height that can be allowed.

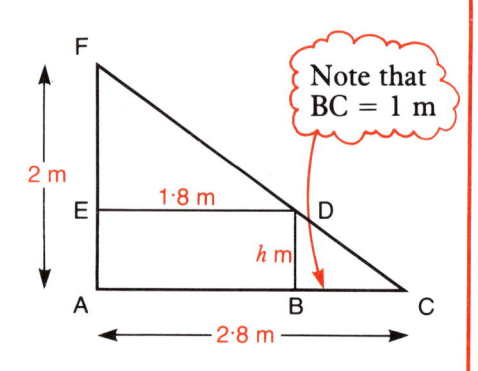

Note that BC = 1 m

2 Show that the triangles are similar.

In triangles CAF and DBC,

$\hat{FAC} = \hat{DBC}$ (both 90°)
$\hat{FCA} = \hat{DCB}$ (common angle)
$\hat{AFC} = \hat{BDC}$ (sum of the angles of a triangle is 180°)

This means that if two of the angles are equal, then the third angles must be equal.

The triangles are equiangular.
Therefore they are similar, and the ratios of the corresponding sides are equal.

3 Draw out the two triangles, write down the equal ratios, and calculate h.

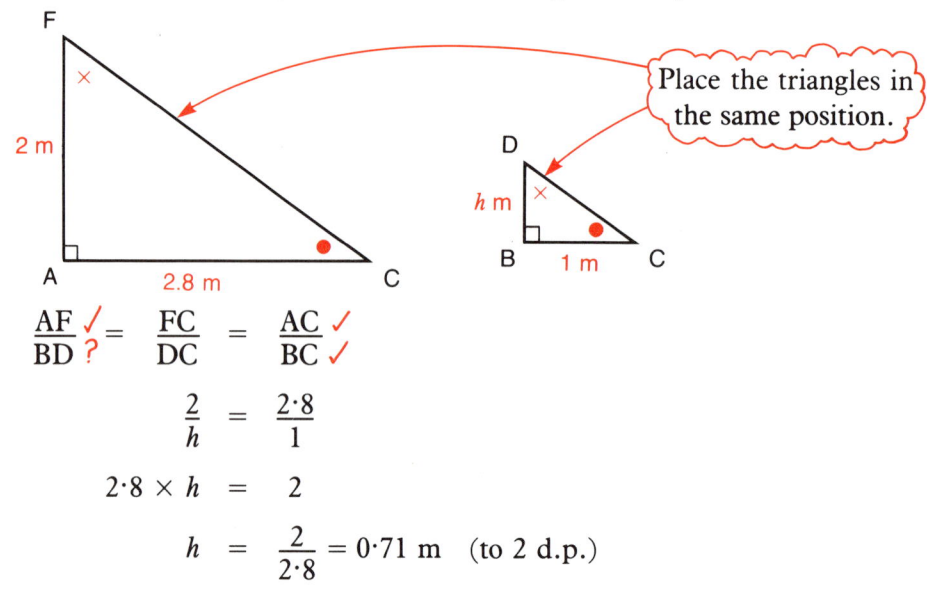

Place the triangles in the same position.

$$\frac{AF}{BD} = \frac{FC}{DC} = \frac{AC}{BC}$$

$$\frac{2}{h} = \frac{2\cdot 8}{1}$$

$$2\cdot 8 \times h = 2$$

$$h = \frac{2}{2\cdot 8} = 0\cdot 71 \text{ m} \quad \text{(to 2 d.p.)}$$

Since the height of the chest of drawers is more than 0·71 m, it will not fit in.

E1 A ladder reaches 3·6 m up the wall of a house and its base is 2·1 m out from the bottom of the wall.

What is the furthest away from the wall that a man of height 1·8 m can walk under the ladder without having to bend down?

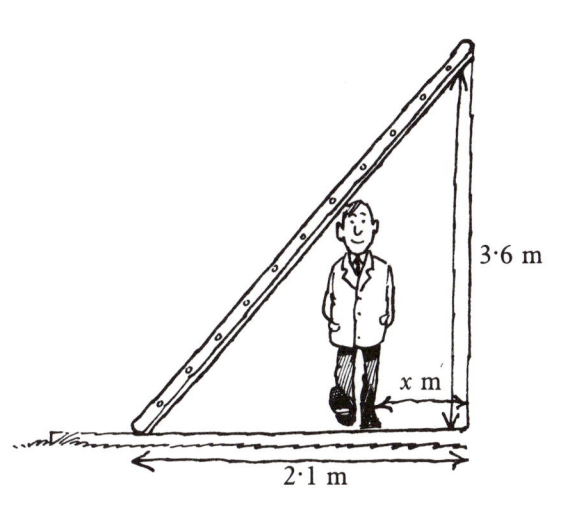

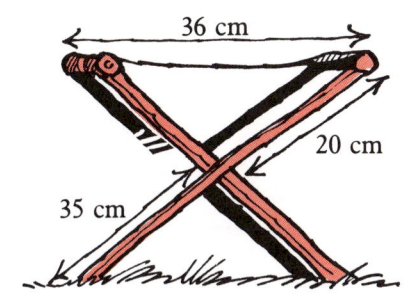

E2 How far apart are the feet of this camp stool?

E3 A father and son are standing outside on a sunny day.

The father is 1·8 m tall and has a shadow 3 m long. If the boy is 1·2 m tall, how long is his shadow?

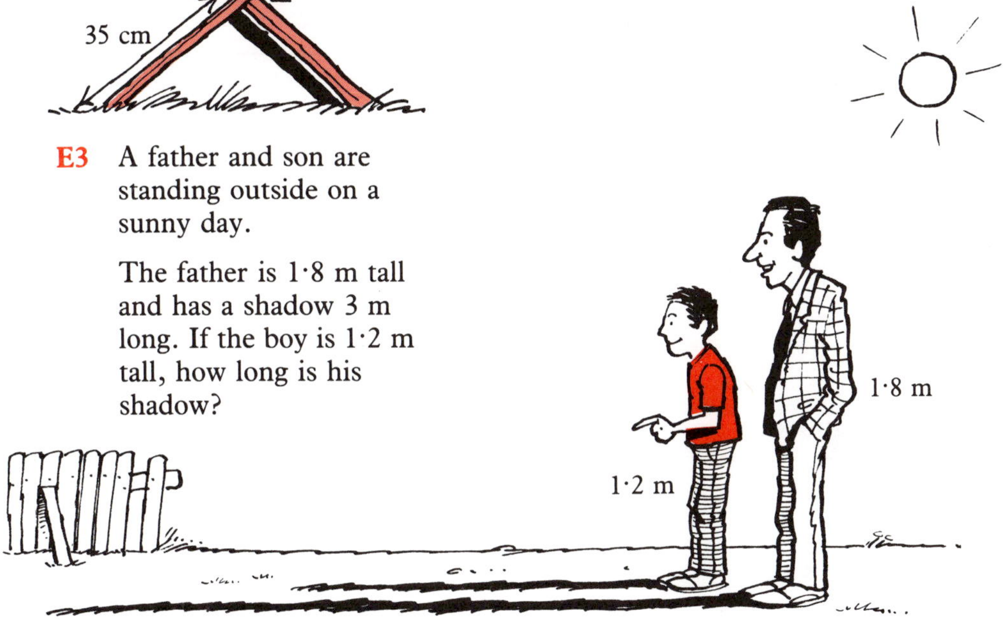

E4 The sign outside Jill's Café keeps falling down and a metal stay is to be fixed half-way down.

If the boards are 1·6 m high and they are 70 cm apart at the bottom, what is the distance between the boards at the point where the stay will be fixed?

E5 A Girl Guide is trying to calculate the height of a building using a metre ruler and a piece of wood 2 cm long.

She lines the metre stick up horizontally and moves the piece of wood along it until its end is in her line of sight from the end of the ruler to the top of the building.

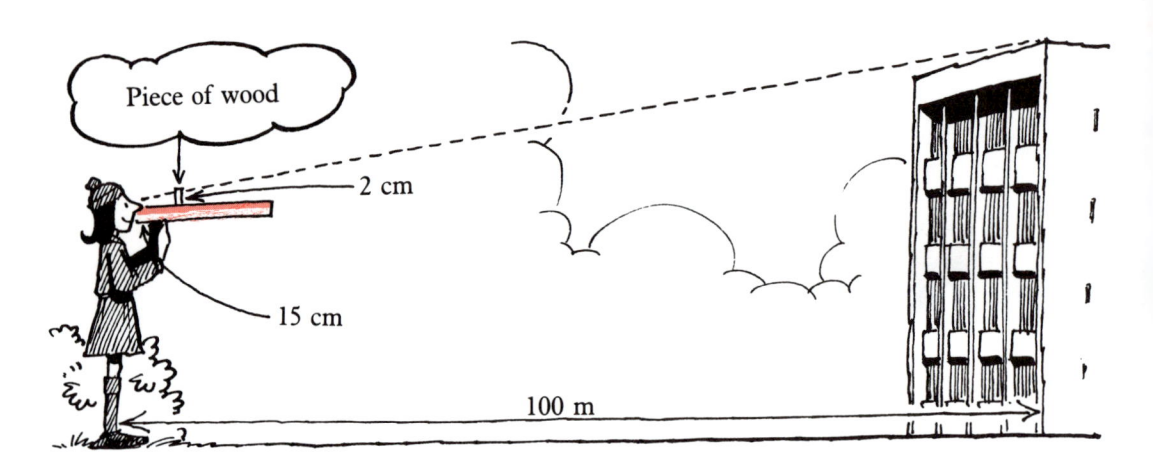

If she is 100 m away from the building and the piece of wood has to be placed 15 cm from the end of the ruler, calculate the height of the building.

Why is this less than the true height of the building, and how could you compensate for this?

Graphs (1)

1. Evaluate each of these quadratic functions for values of x from -1 to $+3$.
   - (a) $f(x) = x^2 - 2x + 4$
   - (b) $f(x) = (x + 2)(x - 5)$
   - (c) $f(x) = 3x^2 + 2x - 7$
   - (d) $f(x) = -4x^2 - 9x + 5$

2. Draw the graph of each of the following functions for the values of x stated.
   - (a) $f(x) = 4x^2 - 36$ $-4 \leqslant x \leqslant 4$
   - (b) $f(x) = 2x^2 + 2x - 12$ $-3 \leqslant x \leqslant 3$

3. Where does the function $f(x) = (x + 5)(x - 4)$ cross the x-axis?

4. What is the maximum value of $49 - x^2$ for $-8 \leqslant x \leqslant 8$?

5. What is the minimum value of the function $f(x) = x^2 - 3x - 10$ for values of x between -3 and $+6$?

6. Alan is building a path of even width, x m, around the rectangular lawn in his garden.

   (a) By splitting the path up into squares and rectangles, work out a formula for the area of the path, $A(x)$.

   (b) On 2 mm graph paper draw a graph of the function $A(x)$ for $x = 0, \frac{1}{2}, 1, \ldots 4$.

   (c) For what value of x will the path have the same area as the lawn?

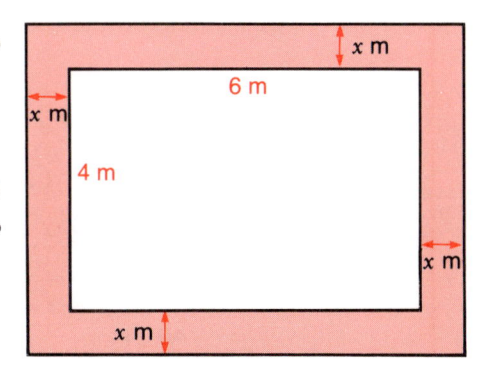

Hire purchase and VAT

1. This guitar can be bought at a cash price of £299·99 or on hire purchase for 100 weeks at £3·70 per week.

   Calculate how much interest is paid if the guitar is bought on hire purchase.

2   This gold necklace can be bought on hire purchase for 100 weeks at £2·71 or at a cash price which is £50·76 lower.

   Calculate the cash price of the necklace.

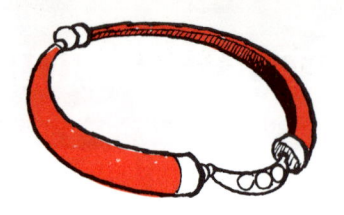

3   This cooker can be bought for a cash price of £449·95 or on one of two hire purchase schemes.

   (a) One scheme is over one year, with equal weekly payments and an annual interest rate of 22%. Calculate the cost of one weekly payment under this scheme.

   (b) The other scheme has 100 weekly payments of £5·54. Calculate the total hire purchase price under this scheme.

   (c) Under which of the schemes is more interest charged?

4   These bills do not include VAT.

   Copy and complete them.

   ```
   2 soups        £1·50
   Steak Pie      £2·95
   Prawn Salad    £3·50
                  ─────
        TOTAL    £7·95
   VAT (15%)     _____
        TOTAL    _____
   ```

   ```
   1 Pate       £1·25
   1 Soup         75p
   1 Steak      £5·20
   1 Chicken    £2·95
                ──────
        TOTAL  £10·15
   VAT (15%)   _____
        TOTAL  _____
   ```

5   These bills do include VAT.

   Copy and complete them.

   ```
   Mr Smith
   DIY materials


   VAT (15%)  £2·48
        TOTAL  _____
   ```

   ```
   Miss McDonald
   Materials


   VAT (15%)  _____
        TOTAL  £8·34
   ```

Angles greater than 90°

1 Find two possible values for x in each of these equations.
(a) $\sin x° = 0·632$
(b) $\cos x° = -0·231$
(c) $\tan x° = -4·9$
(d) $\cos x° = -0·983$
(e) $\sin x° = \dfrac{1}{\sqrt{2}}$
(f) $\cos x° = -\dfrac{\sqrt{3}}{2}$
(g) $\tan x° = -\sqrt{3}$
(h) $\sin x° = \tfrac{1}{2}$

2 Prove each of the following identities.
(a) $3 \sin^2 x° = 3 - 3 \cos^2 x°$
(b) $5 \tan x° \cos x° = 5 \sin x°$
(c) $\dfrac{\sin x°}{\cos(90° - x°)} + 1 = 2$
(d) $\dfrac{\sin x°}{\tan x°} = \sin(90° - x°)$

3 Solve each of the following equations, for $0° \leq x° \leq 360°$.
(a) $2 \cos x° = 0·5$
(b) $3 \sin x° - 1 = 0·72$
(c) $4 \cos x° + 2 = 0·75$
(d) $\tfrac{1}{2} \tan x° + 4 = 3$
(e) $0·3 \sin x° = -0·01$
(f) $0·75 \cos x° = -0·25$
(g) $2 \tan x° = \dfrac{2}{\sqrt{2}}$
(h) $2 \cos x° = -1$
(i) $3 \cos x° + 1 = -2$
(j) $\sin x° + 1 = \dfrac{2 + \sqrt{3}}{2}$

Savings and investment

1 Denise has £750 to invest. She wants to put it into a bank or building society account for two years.

Which of the following accounts will pay her the most interest at the end of the two years?

    A Reidland Bank: $7\tfrac{1}{2}$% interest per annum (simple interest)
    B Millerway Building Society: 7% interest, compounded annually
    C Sureloan Building Society: 7% interest, compounded six-monthly

2 Castle Life shares were on sale at 230p each.
(a) How many shares in the company could William get for £525?
(b) If the yield was 5·3%, calculate William's expected dividend.

Similar triangles

1 Explain why each of the following pairs of triangles is equiangular, and calculate the lengths of the sides indicated.

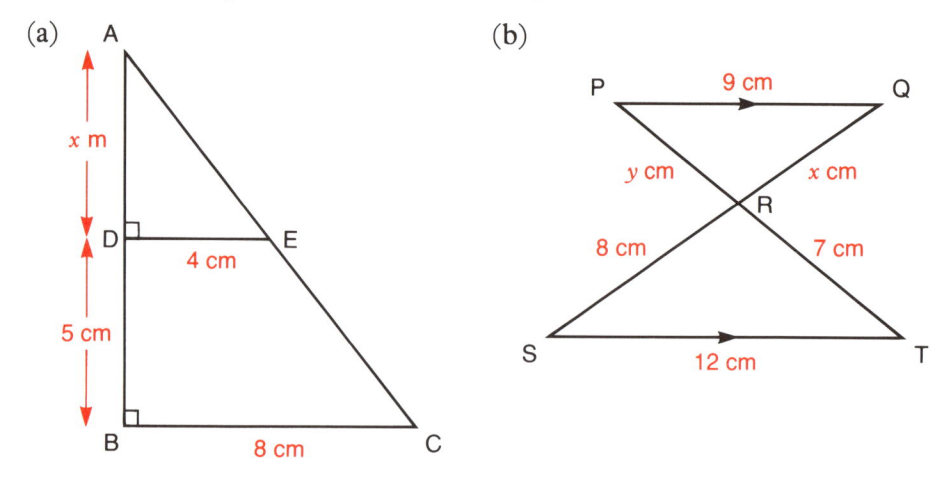

(a) Triangles ADE and ABC.
Calculate AB.

(b) Triangles PQR and RST.
Calculate PR and QR.

2 A pantograph is a drawing instrument which can be used to enlarge or reduce pictures.

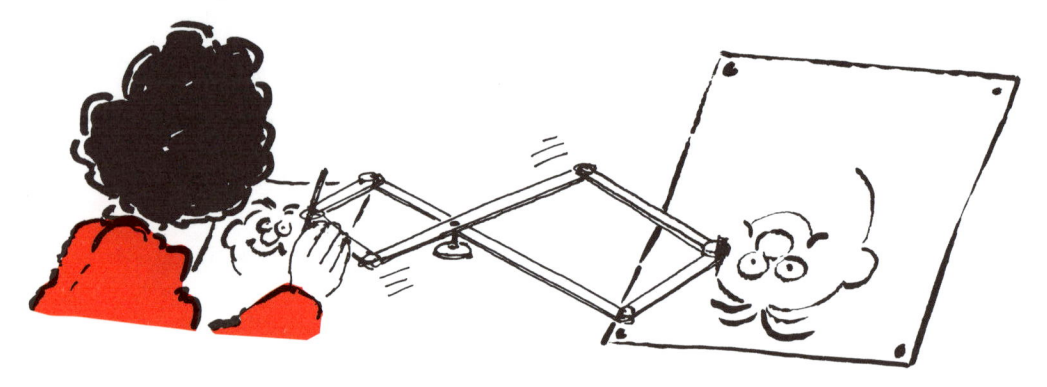

The shape drawn by the machine is similar to the original but it is drawn upside-down.

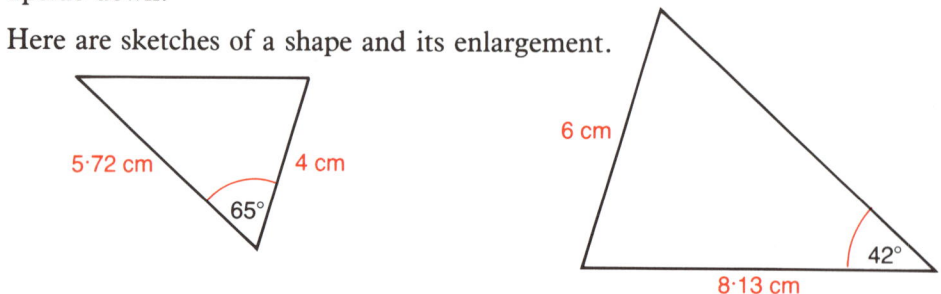

Here are sketches of a shape and its enlargement.

Calculate the sizes of all the unlabelled angles and sides.

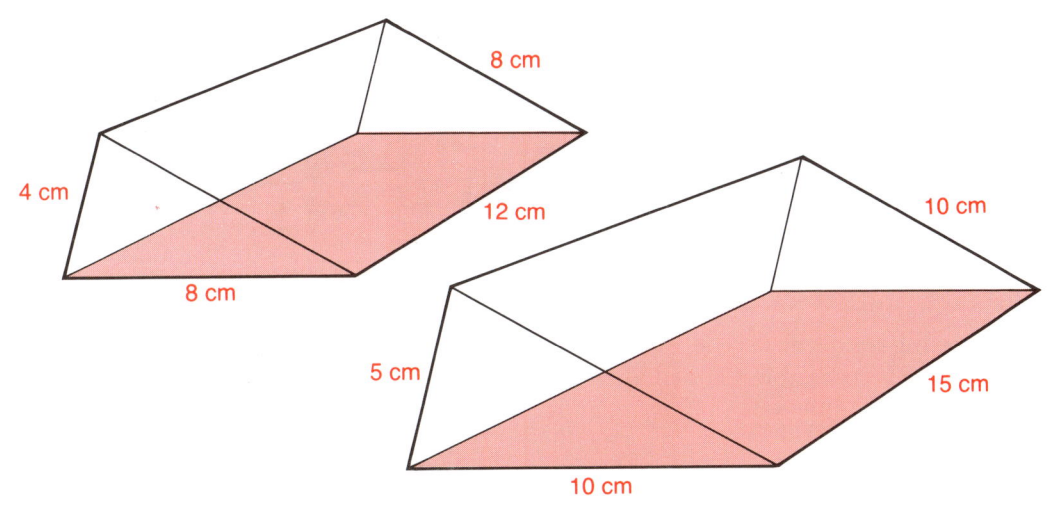

3 Write down the ratios of
  (a) the sides
  (b) the surface areas
  (c) the volumes of the two prisms.

7 The cosine rule

A The problem

Alastair is making a model fort for his son.

There is a drawbridge at the front, and Alastair has to calculate how much string he needs, if the drawbridge is to be able to open at an angle of 125°.

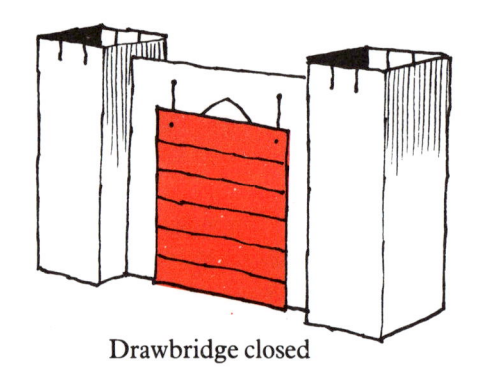

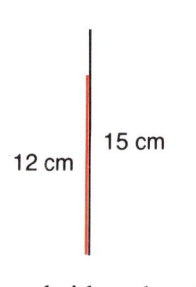

Drawbridge closed

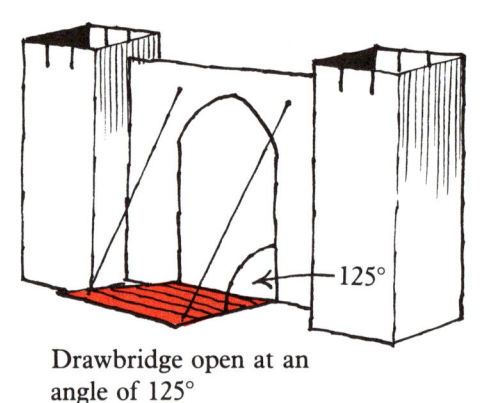

Drawbridge open at an angle of 125°

Looking at this 'sideways on':

12 cm   15 cm

Drawbridge closed

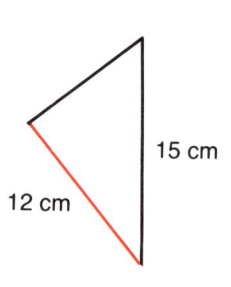

15 cm   12 cm

Drawbridge partly open

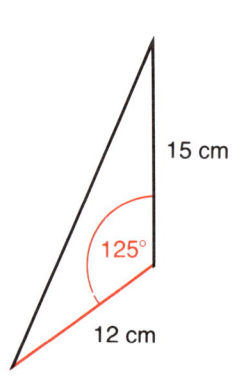

15 cm   125°   12 cm

Drawbridge fully open

Obviously the amount of string Alastair needs depends on the angle between the drawbridge and the wall. Suppose the drawbridge only needed to open to an angle of 40°.

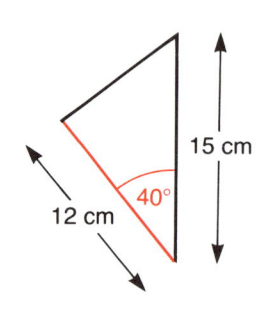

12 cm   40°   15 cm

Here is one way Alastair could work out the length of string he would need then.

Draw in the dotted line and label the diagram.

Using triangle ACD we can work out the lengths of CD and AD.

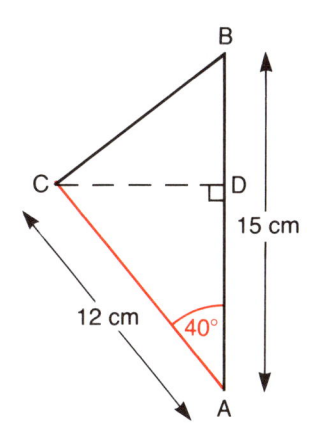

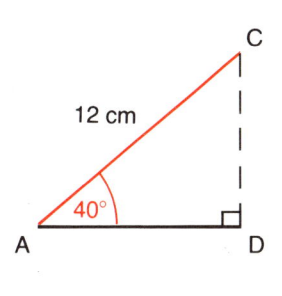

A1 Copy and complete the following working.

sin 40° = . . .   cos 40° = . . .
0·643 = ... = . . .
CD = . . . cm   AD = . . . cm

So now the diagram looks like this.

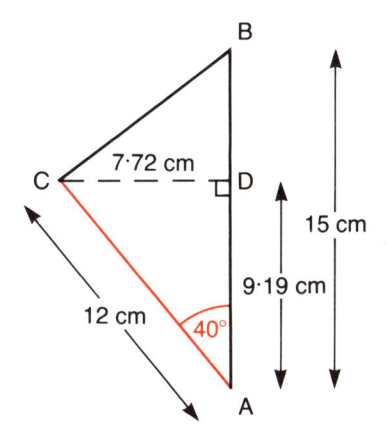

A2 What length is BD?

A3 Using triangle BCD and Pythagoras' rule, calculate the length of BC.

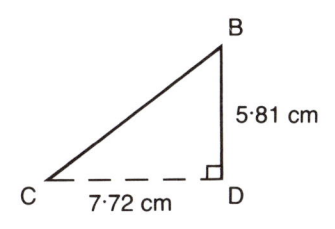

Let's try doing that for a triangle with *any* acute angle and *any* sides.

1 Draw a diagram.

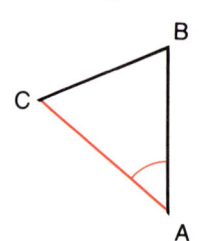

2 Label the sides.

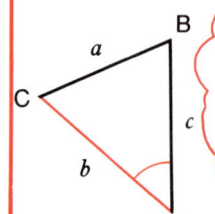

The side opposite vertex A is called a, the one opposite vertex B is b, and the one opposite vertex C is c.

3 Draw in the dotted line.

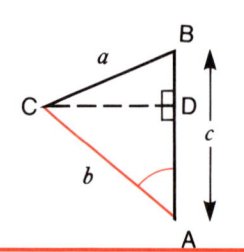

4 Take triangle ACD and work out CD and AD.

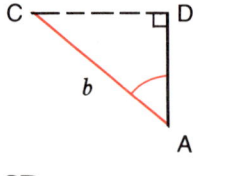

$$\sin \hat{A} = \frac{CD}{b} \qquad \cos \hat{A} = \frac{AD}{b}$$

$$CD = b \sin \hat{A} \qquad AD = b \cos \hat{A}$$

5 Mark in CD and AD.

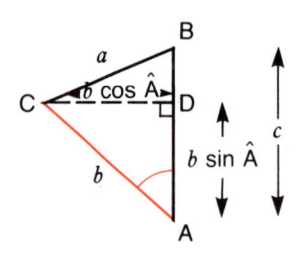

6 Work out BD and use Pythagoras' rule in triangle BCD.

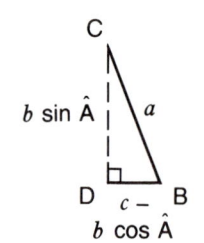

$$\begin{aligned}
a^2 &= (b \sin \hat{A})^2 + (c - b \cos \hat{A})^2 \\
&= b^2 \sin^2 \hat{A} + c^2 - 2bc \cos \hat{A} + b^2 \cos^2 \hat{A} \\
&= b^2 \sin^2 \hat{A} + b^2 \cos^2 \hat{A} + c^2 - 2bc \cos \hat{A} \\
&= b^2(\sin^2 \hat{A} + \cos^2 \hat{A}) + c^2 - 2bc \cos \hat{A}
\end{aligned}$$

$$a^2 = b^2 + c^2 - 2bc \cos \hat{A}$$

This equals 1.

B The obtuse-angled case

Now consider the drawbridge in the fully open position.

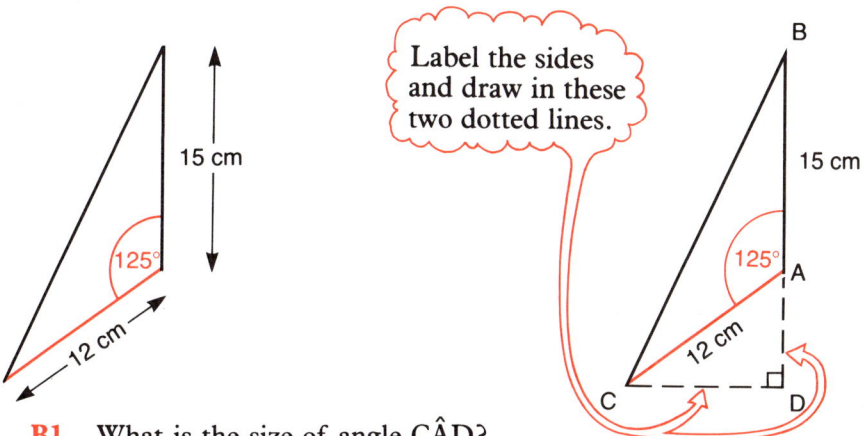

Label the sides and draw in these two dotted lines.

B1 What is the size of angle CÂD? (Use triangle ACD.)

Using triangle ACD we can work out the lengths of CD and AD.

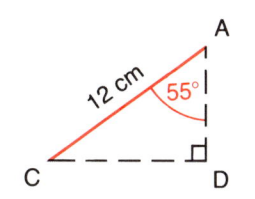

B2 Copy and complete the following working.

$\sin 55° = \ldots$ $\qquad$ $\cos 55° = \ldots$
$0{\cdot}819 = \ldots$ $\qquad$ $\ldots = \ldots$
$CD = \ldots$ cm $\qquad$ $AD =$ cm

So now our diagram looks like this.

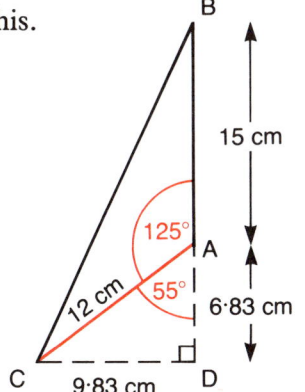

B3 What length is BD?

B4 Using triangle BCD and Pythagoras' rule, calculate the length of BC. (Draw a diagram to help you.)

107

Here is the working for *any* obtuse-angled triangle.

1 Draw and label a diagram.

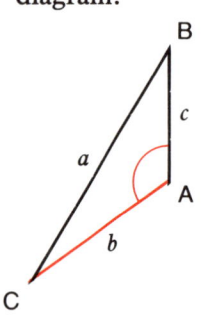

2 Draw in the dotted line.

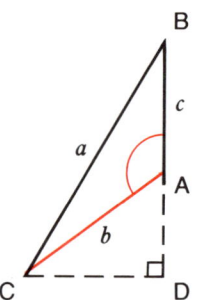

3 Find $\cos(180° - \hat{A})$ and $\sin(180° - \hat{A})$.

$\cos(180° - \hat{A}) = -\cos \hat{A}$
So $\cos C\hat{A}D = -\cos \hat{A}$
$\sin(180° - \hat{A}) = \sin \hat{A}$
so $\sin C\hat{A}D = \sin \hat{A}$

4 Take triangle ACD and calculate AD and CD.

$$\sin C\hat{A}D = \frac{CD}{b} \qquad \cos C\hat{A}D = \frac{AD}{b}$$

$$CD = b \sin C\hat{A}D \qquad AD = b \cos C\hat{A}D$$

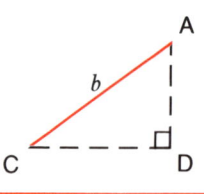

5 Mark in CD and AD.

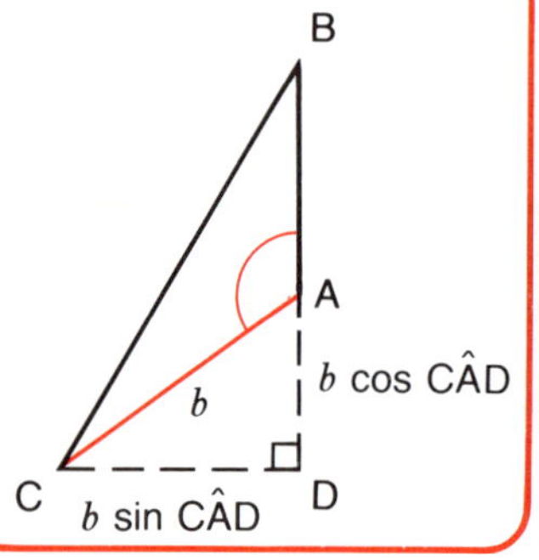

6 Work out BD and use Pythagoras' rule in triangle BCD.

$$\begin{aligned}
a^2 &= (b \sin C\hat{A}D)^2 + (c + b \cos C\hat{A}D)^2 \\
&= b^2 \sin^2 C\hat{A}D + c^2 + 2bc \cos C\hat{A}D + b^2 \cos^2 C\hat{A}D \\
&= b^2 \sin^2 C\hat{A}D + b^2 \cos^2 C\hat{A}D + c^2 + 2bc \cos C\hat{A}D \\
&= b^2(\sin^2 C\hat{A}D + \cos^2 C\hat{A}D) + c^2 + 2bc \cos C\hat{A}D \\
&= b^2 + c^2 + 2bc \cos C\hat{A}D
\end{aligned}$$

But $\cos C\hat{A}D = -\cos \hat{A}$ (from step 3)
so $a^2 = b^2 + c^2 - 2bc \cos \hat{A}$

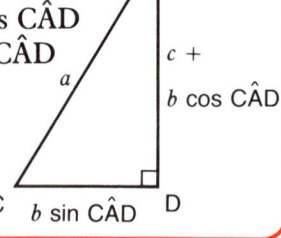

C The right-angled case

This time our drawbridge diagram looks like this.

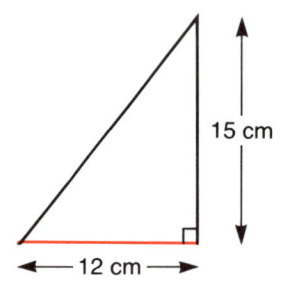

C1 Calculate the length of string required, using Pythagoras' rule.

If you look back at the working for the 'any-angled' triangles in sections A and B, you will find that in both cases

$$a^2 = b^2 + c^2 - 2bc \cos \hat{A}$$

Does this rule work here?

C2 Assume that the rule does work, and copy and complete the following working for the triangle ABC.

$$\begin{aligned} a^2 &= b^2 + c^2 - 2bc \cos \hat{A} \\ &= 12^2 + 15^2 - 2 \times 12 \times 15 \times \cos 90° \\ &= 144 + \ldots - 2 \times 12 \times 15 \times 0 \\ &= \ldots \end{aligned}$$

So $a = \ldots$ cm

Value of a obtained in question C1 = ... cm.

Did the formula hold here?

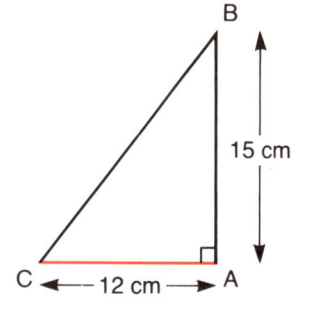

D Using the formula to find a side of a triangle

The formula $a^2 = b^2 + c^2 - 2bc \cos \hat{A}$ is called the **cosine rule**. As we have seen, it works in any triangle.

There is a pattern in the letters:

$$a^2 \quad = \quad b^2 + c^2 \quad - \quad 2bc \quad \times \quad \cos \hat{A}$$

- The side to be found, squared
- = The other two sides, squared and added
- − 2× Other two sides, multiplied together
- × Angle opposite the side to be found

D1 Write down the correct form of the cosine rule to find the given side in each of these triangles.

(a) Side b in triangle ABC
(b) Side c in triangle ABC
(c) Side p in triangle PQR
(d) Side e in triangle DEF
(e) Side z in triangle XYZ
(f) Side f in triangle AFT
(g) Side s in triangle YMS

Worked example

Calculate the length of side PR in triangle PQR.

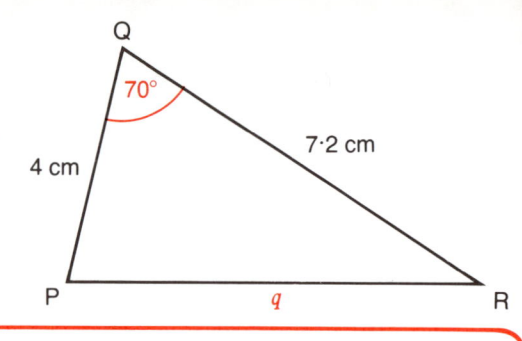

[Triangle PQR with Q at top, angle 70° at Q, PQ = 4 cm, QR = 7.2 cm, side PR = q, right angle at P]

1 Write down the correct form of the cosine rule.

We want to find side q in triangle PQR, so

$q^2 = p^2 + r^2 - 2pr \cos \hat{Q}$

2 Substitute into the rule and solve for q.

$q^2 = p^2 + r^2 - 2pr \cos \hat{Q}$
$= 7·2^2 + 4^2 - (2 \times 7·2 \times 4 \times \cos 70°)$
$= 51·84 + 16 - (2 \times 7·2 \times 4 \times 0·342)$
$= 67·84 - 19·70$
$q^2 = 48·14$
$q = 6·938$
So PR = 6·94 (to 3 s.f.)

We work to 4 s.f. during the calculation, and round to 3 s.f. at the end.

D2 Calculate the lengths of the sides marked with letters in each of these triangles. Set out your working as in the worked example above.

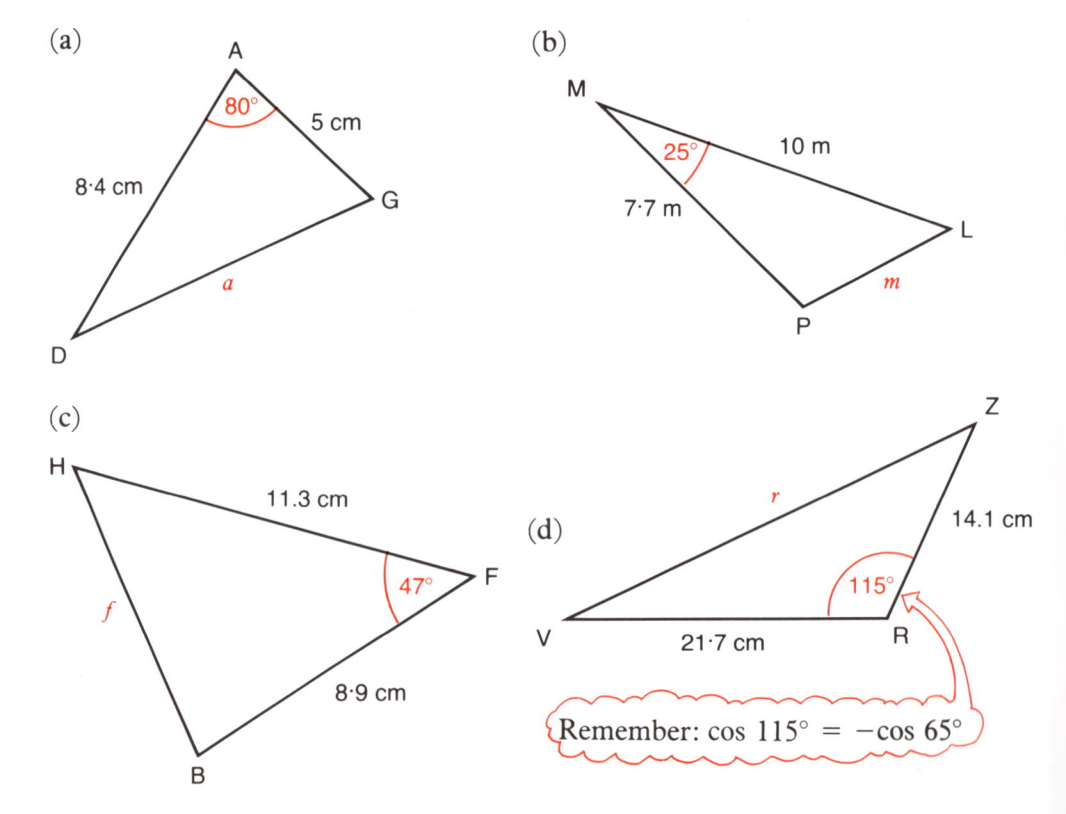

(a) [Triangle with A at top, angle 80° at A, AG = 5 cm, AD = 8.4 cm, side a between D and G]

(b) [Triangle with angle 25° at M, ML = 10 m, MP = 7.7 m, side m between P and L]

(c) [Triangle with angle 47° at F, HF = 11.3 cm, FB = 8.9 cm, side f between H and B]

(d) [Triangle with angle 115° at R, VR = 21.7 cm, RZ = 14.1 cm, side r between V and Z]

Remember: $\cos 115° = -\cos 65°$

110

(e)

T — 7·1 m — S, angle 152°, Y to T = 5·9 m, side t from Y to S

(f)

Triangle DEF: DE = 8·1 cm, DF = 10·6 cm, angle D = 37°, EF = d

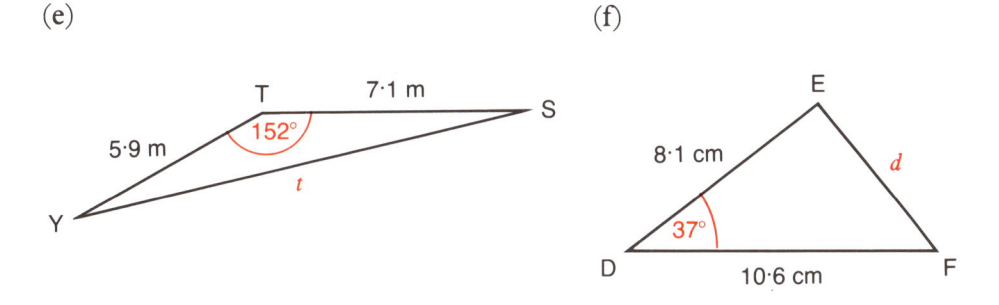

D3 The minute hand and the hour hand of Big Ben are 4·27 m and 2·74 m long respectively.

Calculate the straight-line distance between the tips of the hands at

(a) 14.00   (b) 09.30   (c) 16.10

D4 The ventilator window in a greenhouse opens to an angle of 38°.

The ventilator is 60 cm long, and it is supported by a prop attached 40 cm down from the hinge.

Calculate the length of the support.

D5 Two Legionnaires leave a fort at the same time. One walks on a bearing of 077° for 130 km and the other on a bearing of 324° for 85 km.

Calculate how far apart the Legionnaires will be at the ends of their journeys.

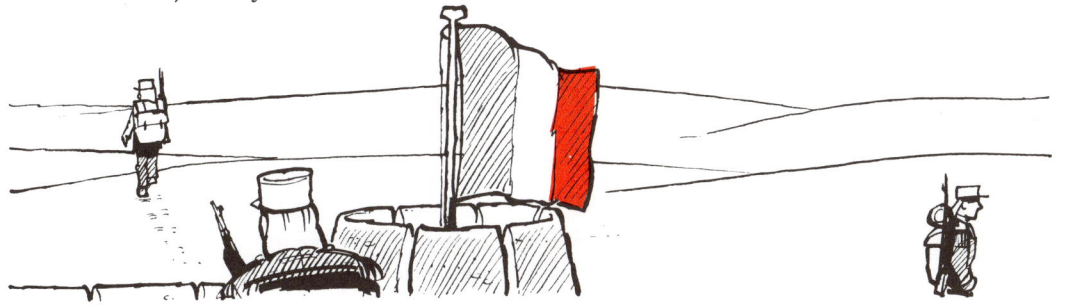

D6 The SS *Ahoy* leaves Leith docks and sails for 100 km on a bearing of 065°. It then changes course and sails for a further 170 km on a bearing of 153°.

Calculate how far it will be from Leith docks at the end of its journey.

D7 Two explorers, Iris Lookforit and Stephen Earch set off from base camp in different directions.

Miss Lookforit goes on a bearing of 018° for 5 km and Mr Earch goes on a bearing of 140° for 7 km.

Calculate how far apart they end up.

E Finding an angle in a triangle, given its three sides

The cosine rule for finding side a in triangle ABC is

$a^2 = b^2 + c^2 - 2bc \cos \hat{A}$

We can re-arrange this so that $\cos \hat{A}$ is the subject.

$2bc \cos \hat{A} = b^2 + c^2 - a^2$

$\cos \hat{A} = \dfrac{b^2 + c^2 - a^2}{2bc}$

Notice the pattern:

$$\cos (\text{angle}) = \frac{(\text{Other two sides, squared and added}) - (\text{Side opposite angle, squared})}{2 \times (\text{Other two sides, multiplied together})}$$

E1 Write down the correct version of the cosine rule to find the given angle in each of these triangles.

(a) $\hat{B}$ in triangle ABC
(b) $\hat{C}$ in triangle ABC
(c) $\hat{P}$ in triangle PTR
(d) $\hat{D}$ in triangle ADT
(e) $\hat{Q}$ in triangle QBA
(f) $\hat{H}$ in triangle GBH

Worked example

Calculate the size of $\hat{P}$ in triangle SPM, where SP = 3·9 cm, PM = 7·6 cm and SM = 8·1 cm.

1 Write down the correct form of the cosine rule.

We want to find $\hat{P}$ in triangle SPM, so

$$\cos \hat{P} = \frac{s^2 + m^2 - p^2}{2sm}$$

2 Substitute into the formula and solve for $\hat{P}$.

$$\cos \hat{P} = \frac{s^2 + m^2 - p^2}{2sm}$$

$$= \frac{7\cdot6^2 + 3\cdot9^2 - 8\cdot1^2}{2 \times 7\cdot6 \times 3\cdot9}$$

$$= \frac{57\cdot76 + 15\cdot21 - 65\cdot61}{59\cdot28}$$

$$= \frac{7\cdot36}{59\cdot28}$$

$$= 0\cdot124 \quad \text{(to 3 s.f.)}$$

So $\hat{P} = 82\cdot9°$

E2 Calculate the sizes of the angles marked in each of these triangles. Set out your working as in the worked example above.

(a)

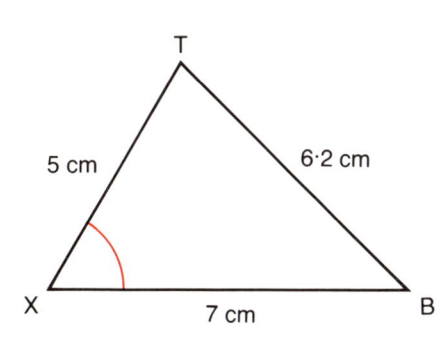

(b)

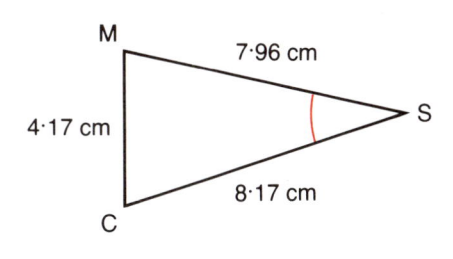

(c)

P — 62·3 cm — Z
48·2 cm, 57 cm, D

(d)

V
12·7 cm
14·7 cm
Q
13·4 cm
E

(e)

F
5·08 cm, 7·16 cm
K — 4·71 cm — R

(f)

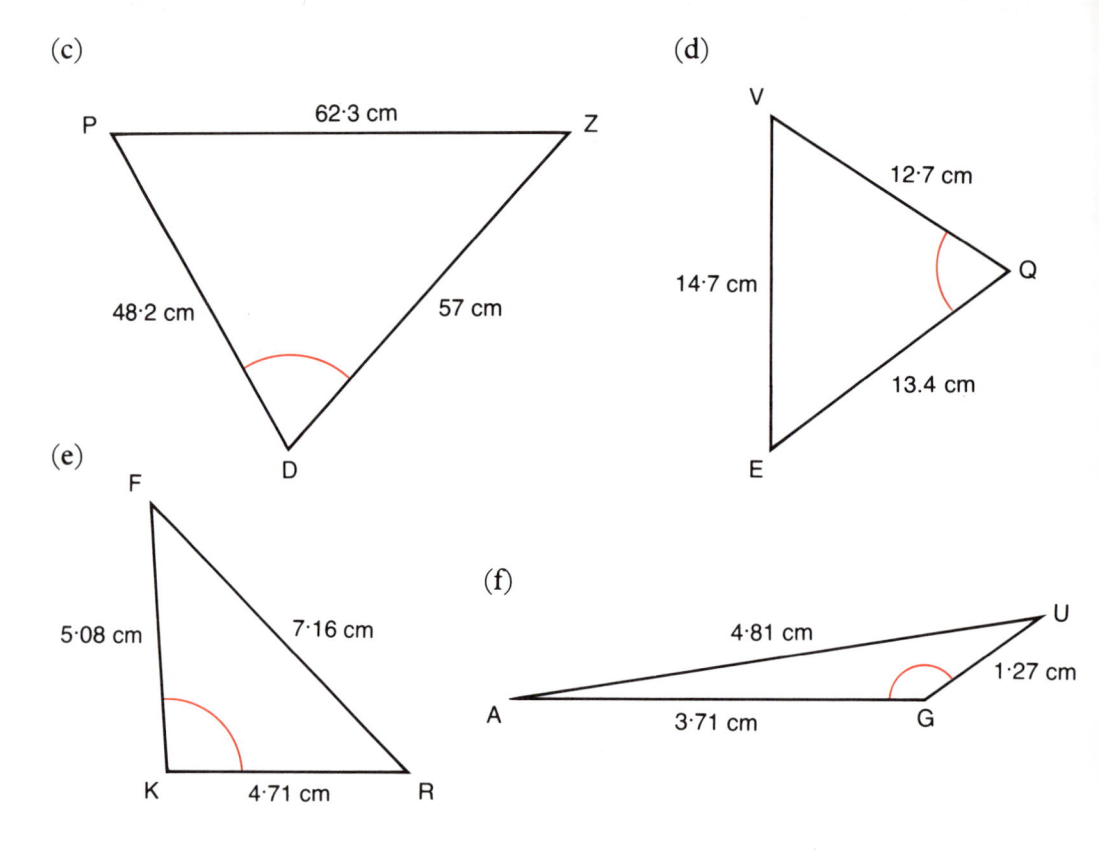

A — 3·71 cm — G, 4·81 cm, 1·27 cm — U

E3 A golfer standing 240 m from the hole hits a drive 210 m. But the ball is still 50 m short of the hole.

Calculate the angle which his drive made with the direction of the hole.

E4 Calculate the largest angle in a triangle whose sides are 4·7 cm, 5·9 cm and 5·1 cm.

E5 (a) A picture is hung from its corners by a piece of string 58 cm long. If the width of the picture is 40 cm and it is hung lop-sided, so that 32 cm of string is on one side and 26 cm of string on the other, calculate the angle between the two parts of the string.

(b) Also calculate the angle between the two parts of the string if the picture is hung so that it is horizontal. (You can do this in two ways – try both of them.)

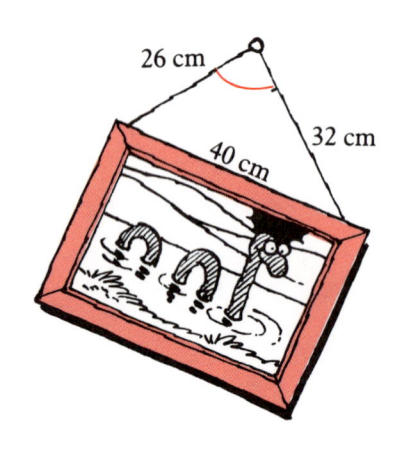

Money management 5: Loans and insurance

A Loans

Colin has decided to buy this car. He cannot afford to pay for it all at once, so he asks the garage for details of their loan scheme. He wants to know how much interest he must pay, and how much the monthly payments will be.

Here are the details the garage gives him:

Willit Start & Sons Ltd

CAR LOAN SCHEME

Conditions

Minimum deposit 10%

Balance to be paid over three years at interest rate of 11% per annum

Example: £350 Deposit

Amount borrowed	£3150.00
First year's interest	£346.50
Amount owed, beginning of second year	£3496.50
Second year's interest	£384.62
Amount owed, beginning of third year	£3881.12
Third year's interest	£426.91
Total owed	£4308.03
36 monthly payments of	£119.67
Total interest charged	£1158.03

A1 Colin decides to go ahead with the loan, and pays a deposit of £500.

Calculate his monthly payments.

A2 Anna Sharp has decided to buy a second-hand car that costs £1960. She pays a deposit of £100 and takes out a loan with the Trusty Finance Company at 9·07% interest per annum.

(a) If she pays off the loan in monthly instalments over two years, how much will she pay each month?

(b) If she pays off the loan over three years, how much more interest will she have to pay?

A3 Victor Peters has bought a new Roadstar sports car for £9750. He pays a deposit of 25% of the car's value, and repays the rest to a finance company at an interest rate of 9·15% per annum.

(a) If he wants to pay off the loan over five years, work out his monthly payments and the total interest paid.

(b) How much will Victor have to pay if he decides to pay off the rest of the loan after two years?

(**Remember:** He will already have made 24 payments.)

A4 Julia Stone is buying her first car. She wants to be sure that she can afford the repayments every month, but wants to repay the loan as soon as possible.

She has calculated that she can afford a deposit of no more than £250 and payments of no more than £125 per month.

Which of the following deals would suit Julia best?

Give reasons for your answer.

A Garageloan Ltd: £200 deposit
 Pay balance at 9·98% per annum over three years
B Lowland Bank: 7% deposit
 Pay balance over two, three or four years at 11·2% per annum
C Carcash plc: Deposit 10% of cash price
 Balance payable over five years at 9·24% interest per annum

B Other types of loan

Loans can also be taken out with finance companies and banks for other items, such as holidays, furniture, home improvements, and so on. The interest charged varies from company to company.

Here are some examples for you to try.

B1 Sandra takes out a loan of £1050 with her bank to install double glazing in her home. The bank charges an interest rate of 9·98% per annum. Sandra repays the loan over three years.

(a) Calculate the total interest charged.

(b) Calculate her monthly payments.

B2 Brian wants to start up in his own window cleaning business. To do this he needs to take out a loan for £750.

Which of the following schemes do you think is best for Brian?

Give reasons for your answer.

- A Bank of Trust: Annual interest of 10·05%
                        Repayment over two years
- B Friendly Loan plc: Annual interest of 7·4%
                        Repayment over six years
- C Sureloan Ltd: Annual interest of 9·2%
                        Repayment over five years

C Car insurance

Once a car is bought, the driver is required by law to be insured.

Here are the three main types of car insurance that are available.

Type of insurance	Details of accident	Insurance company pays
Third party	*Another* vehicle damaged, or *another* person injured	Cost of repairs to other vehicle, any compensation to injured person
Third party, fire and theft	As above, or *driver's* vehicle is damaged by fire or stolen	As above, also pays out for burnt or stolen vehicle
Comprehensive	As above, or *driver's* vehicle is damaged by fire or stolen	As above, also pays cost of repairs to driver's vehicle

C1 Here are some drawings of car accidents. For each drawing, list the items that would be paid for by the driver's insurance.

(a)

Mr Jones has third party insurance.

117

(b)

Susan Yates caused this accident.
She has third party, fire and theft insurance.

(c)

Mr Firth caused this accident.
He has fully comprehensive insurance.

The amount a driver pays each year is called the **premium**. How much the premium is depends on many factors, such as the type of car, the type of insurance, where the driver lives, and so on.

If the insurance company does not have to pay out anything during a year, the driver is usually given a **no claims bonus**. This means that the insurance premiums for future years are reduced.

This table shows the no claims discounts offered by the Easylife Insurance Company.

Number of years without claim	Discount
1	25%
2	40%
3	50%
4 or more	60%

If the company has to pay out for a claim, the driver loses one year's discount.

C2 William has been driving for three years without a claim. He has a comprehensive insurance policy with an annual premium of £280.

Calculate William's no claims discount.

C3 Anne has been driving for two years without a claim. She pays £180 a year for her insurance.

Calculate the full cost of the premium.

C4 Aileen has been driving for four years without a claim. The annual premium for her car is £369.

(a) What percentage of this premium does Aileen pay?

(b) During this year Aileen has to claim on her insurance.
How much will she have to pay when her next payment is due?

C5 Sidney has been driving for two years without a claim when he reverses into a wall. It would cost £20 to repair the damage to his car.

(a) If the normal premium for his car was £325, how much did Sidney pay with his two years' discount?

(b) If he claims on his insurance for the repairs, he will lose one year's no claims discount.

How much would Sidney then have to pay for his insurance?

(c) Do you think Sidney should pay for the repairs himself or claim on his insurance?

Give a reason for your answer.

D House insurance

Another common type of insurance is house insurance. This covers a building and its contents. Householders can be insured against theft, fire, damage to the building by storms, and so on.

The premium payable depends on where the house is, and on the value of the house and its contents.

This table shows the rates charged by the Diamond Star Insurance Group.

Annual premium for every £100 insured		
	Building	**Contents**
Urban rate	13p	35p
Rural rate	11p	32p

Worked example

June lives in a small village and wants to insure her cottage, which is worth £37 000, and its contents, which are worth £12 000.

Calculate her annual premium.

Rural rates apply.

Building: 370 × 11p = £40·70
Contents: 120 × 32p = £38·40
   Total premium = £79·10

D1 Calculate the annual insurance premium for each of these houses, if both the building and its contents are to be insured.

(a) House value £47 500
Contents £26 000
Rural rates apply

(b) House value £24 000
Contents £10 000
Urban rates apply

(c) House value £123 000
Contents £75 000
Rural rates apply

D2 Mr Kelly, who lives in Glasgow, pays an annual premium of £73·84 for his house insurance, and £87·50 for the contents insurance.

Calculate the value of his house and its contents.

D3 Mrs Brown and her family used to live in Glasgow, but have recently moved to a cottage on the shores of Loch Lomond. She finds that her insurance premium for the new building is exactly the same as for the old one.

If the premium on her Glasgow house was £114·40, calculate the value of her new house.

8 Patterns

A Sequences

In this chapter we shall deal with patterns of numbers.

A1 Here are some patterns of numbers.

Try to continue each pattern for two more stages.

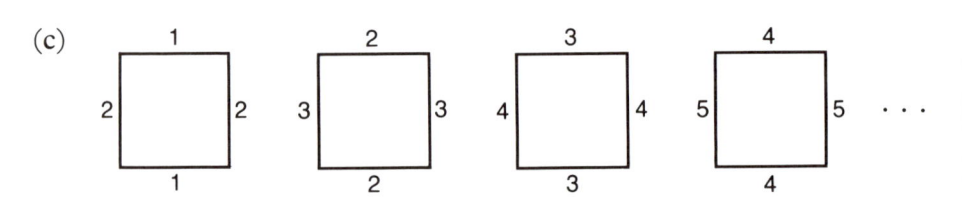

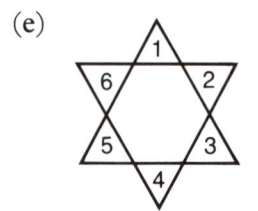

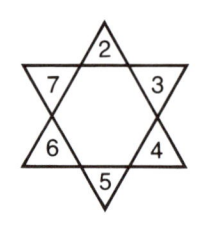

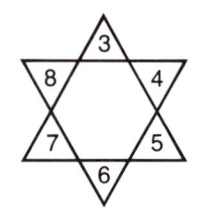

(a)
```
        1           2           3           4
    1       1   2       2   3       3   4       4     . . .
        1           2           3           4
```

(b) 2, 4, 6, 8, . . .

(c) Squares with sides labelled:
- Square 1: 1, 2, 1, 2
- Square 2: 2, 3, 2, 3
- Square 3: 3, 4, 3, 4
- Square 4: 4, 5, 4, 5
. . .

(d) 1, 2, 4, 7, 11, . . .

(e) Six-pointed stars with points numbered:
- Star 1: 1, 2, 3, 4, 5, 6
- Star 2: 2, 3, 4, 5, 6, 7
- Star 3: 3, 4, 5, 6, 7, 8
. . .

(f) 31, 28, 31, 30, 31, . . .

Lists of numbers which are arranged according to a rule are called **sequences**. Each number in a sequence is called a **term** and can be denoted by the letter u.

For example, u_6 is the sixth term, and
u_{19} is the nineteenth term.

A2 Write down u_3 for each of the patterns in question A1.

Often there is a simple rule for going from one term to the next. We call this the 'next-term' rule.

For example, the next-term rule for the sequence 2, 5, 8, 11, . . . is 'add 3'.

A3 For each of the sequences below, calculate the term indicated and write down the next-term rule.

(a) 1, 3, 5, 7, 9, . . . Calculate u_1.

(b) 3, 6, 18, 72, . . . Calculate u_6.

(c) $\frac{1}{2}, \frac{1}{4}, \frac{1}{8}, \ldots$ Calculate u_4.

(d) 1, 0·8, 0·6, 0·4, . . . Calculate u_8.

When you know the next-term rule, you can continue the sequence by applying the rule again and again.

For example, we can calculate u_9 of the sequence

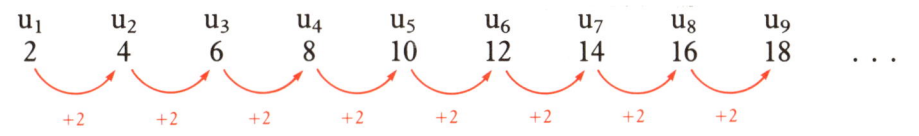

u_1	u_2	u_3	u_4	u_5	u_6	u_7	u_8	u_9	
2	4	6	8	10	12	14	16	18	. . .
+2	+2	+2	+2	+2	+2	+2	+2		

by applying the next-term rule ('add 2') eight times.

Here are some examples for you to try.

A4 Look at this sequence.
5, 10, 15, 20, . . .

(a) Write down the next-term rule.

(b) How many times would you apply the rule to find u_8?

(c) Write down the value of u_8.

A5 Look at this sequence.
100, 97, 94, 91, . . .

(a) Write down the next-term rule.

(b) How many times would you apply the rule to work out u_{25}?

(c) Calculate u_{12}.

A6 Jean gets paid £100 per week. If her wage goes up by £10 a week every year, work out her weekly wage after five years.

A7 Karen's car is losing one-tenth of its value every year. If she bought it for £2500, how much is it worth after three years?

B Flow charts

Flow charts are another way of calculating the terms of a sequence one after another using the next-term rule.

B1 Use this flow chart to write out the values of the terms u_1 to u_5.

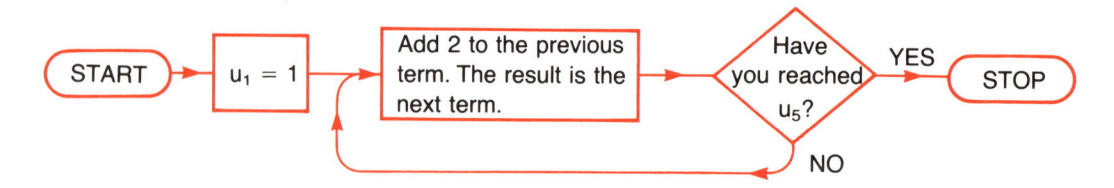

START → $u_1 = 1$ → Add 2 to the previous term. The result is the next term. → Have you reached u_5? — YES → STOP / NO (loop back)

B2 Write down the terms of the sequence produced by this flow chart.

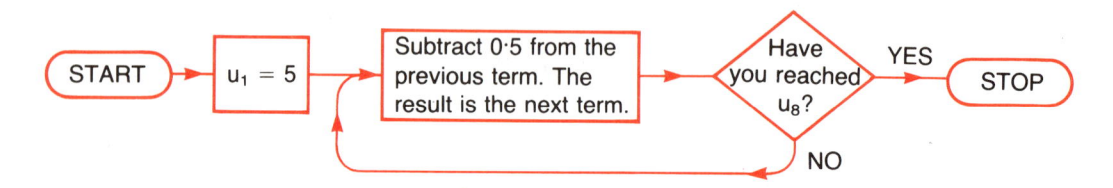

START → $u_1 = 5$ → Subtract 0·5 from the previous term. The result is the next term. → Have you reached u_8? — YES → STOP / NO (loop back)

B3 Write down the terms of the sequence produced by this flow chart.

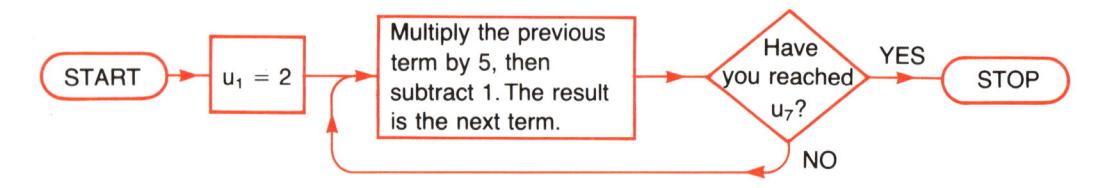

START → $u_1 = 2$ → Multiply the previous term by 5, then subtract 1. The result is the next term. → Have you reached u_7? — YES → STOP / NO (loop back)

B4 Write down the terms of the sequence produced by this flow chart.

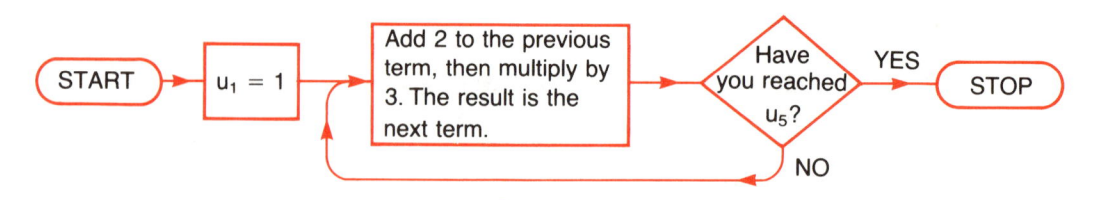

START → $u_1 = 1$ → Add 2 to the previous term, then multiply by 3. The result is the next term. → Have you reached u_5? — YES → STOP / NO (loop back)

Working out the terms of a sequence like this is an example of an iterative process, as we have to go around the loop again and again.

The process becomes quite time consuming if we have to work out a large number of terms to reach the one we want. We shall now look at a quicker way of working out a particular term.

C The 'any-term' rule

Look at this sequence.

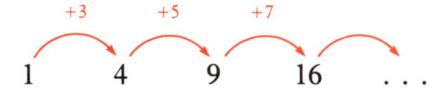

1 →(+3) 4 →(+5) 9 →(+7) 16 ...

We can work out a next-term rule for this sequence but it is a bit more difficult than before, since the amount being added on is getting greater each time.

The rule would be something like 'add 2 extra every time'.

It would be quite difficult to work out u_{99} (for example) using this rule.

Let's look at another way of doing it.

This table shows the positions of the terms in the sequence.

Position	1	2	3	4	
Term	1	4	9	16	

(with arrows ×1, ×2, ×3, ×4 between positions and terms)

We can see that $u_1 = 1^2$
$u_2 = 2^2$
$u_3 = 3^2$
$u_4 = 4^2$

C1 Write down the values of u_9, u_{25} and u_{63}.

C2 Try to write down an expression for u_n.

We call u_n the 'nth term'. The expression which we work out for u_n can then be used to calculate any term in the sequence. We call it the 'any-term' rule, or the 'nth term' rule.

Here is an example.

Position	1	2	3	4	... n	
Term	3	6	9	12	... 3n	$u_n = 3n$

(with ×3 arrows between each position and term)

C3 (a) Calculate u_{57}, u_{949} and u_{1245} for the sequence above.

(b) Which term of the sequence has the value 81?

C4 (a) What is the any-term rule for this sequence?

Position	1	2	3	4	5 ... n
Term	6	12	18	24	30 ...

(b) Calculate u_{24}.

(c) Which term has the value 90?

C5 (a) Find the nth term rule for this sequence.

Position	1	2	3 ... n
Term	5	6	7 ...

(b) Calculate u_{156}.

C6 Here is the nth term rule for a sequence: $u_n = 3n - 1$

Write down the first five terms of the sequence.

C7 Here is the any-term rule for another sequence: $u_n = n(n + 1)$

Write down the first four terms of the sequence.

C8 If $u_n = 2^n$, calculate u_5 and u_{12}.

C9 If $u_n = n^2 - n + 1$, calculate u_1, u_3, u_5 and u_8.

C10 Try to find the nth term rule for each of these sequences.

(a)
Position	1	2	3	4 ... n
Term	3	7	11	15 ...

(**Hint:** Try ×4 first.)

(b)
Position	1	2	3	4 ... n
Term	1	8	27	64 ...

(c)
Position	1	2	3	4 ... n
Term	5	8	11	14 ...

(d)
Position	1	2	3	4 ... n
Term	$\frac{1}{2}$	1	$1\frac{1}{2}$	2 ...

(e)
Position	1	2	3	4 ... n
Term	2	6	12	20 ...

D Problems

D1 This pattern of houses continues along one side of a street.

Work out a rule for the number on the door of the nth tall house.

D2 These patterns are made from red and white square tiles.

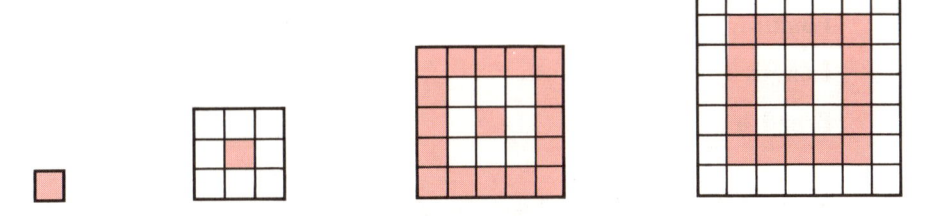

(a) Write down the first four terms of the sequence which gives the total number of tiles needed for each pattern.

(b) Write down u_5 and u_6.

(c) Explain the any-term rule in words.

(d) Write down the any-term rule in symbols.

E Triangular numbers

These patterns of dots give the sequence of triangular numbers.

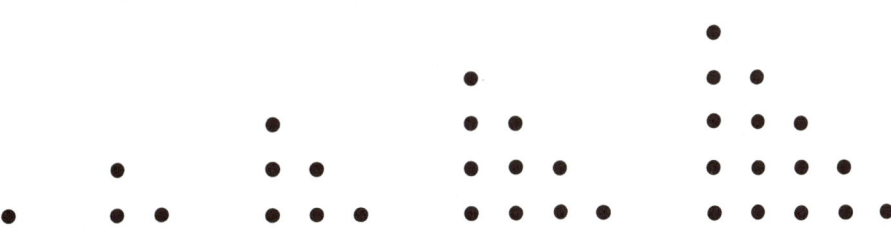

The first triangular number is   1
The second triangular number is $1 + 2 = 3$
The third triangular number is $1 + 2 + 3 = 6$, and so on.

E1 Work out u_{15} and u_{20} using the method above.

If we were to use this method to work out terms such as u_{75} and u_{150}, it could take some time.

We shall now try to find a quicker way.

We can join two sequences of triangular numbers together, to give a sequence of rectangles, like this.

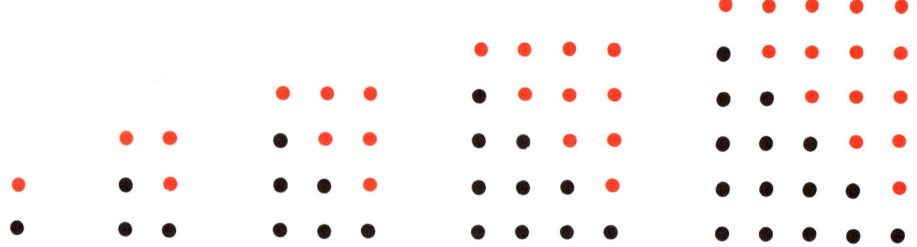

This table shows the dimensions of the rectangles.

Position	1	2	3
Length	2	3	4
Breadth	1	2	3

E2 Write down the dimensions of the 10th rectangle, the 37th rectangle, and the *n*th rectangle.

E3 Copy and complete the table below to show the total number of dots in each rectangle.

Position	1	2	3	4 ... 10 ... 37 ... n
Dots	2	6		

E4 Explain in words how you would obtain the sequence of triangular numbers from the sequence of the number of dots in each rectangle.

E5 Write in symbols the any-term rule for the sequence of triangular numbers.

E6 Use your rule to work out u_{75} and u_{130}.

E7 Which triangular number has the value

(a) 1830 (b) 497

F Investigations

F1 In tennis, an 'American' tournament is one where each player plays a match against every other player.

(a) How many matches would be needed for five players?

(b) Look at how many matches are needed for some other numbers of players.

(c) Can you find a rule that the organisers can use to know how many matches are needed for any number of players?

(d) Find out some other ways that tennis tournaments can be organised. Look at the number of matches needed for different numbers of players.

F2 In a quiz competition, there are two prizes that can be won.

(a) If three teams enter, in how many ways can the prizes be won?

(b) Look at the number of ways the prizes can be won for different numbers of teams.

(c) Look at what happens if different numbers of prizes can be won.

9 Variation

You have already met the terms 'direct proportionality' and 'inverse proportionality'. In this chapter we shall spend some time looking at these again and at how we can translate them into the language of variation.

A Direct variation

Suppose that books cost £3 each. This table shows how the total cost (£C) varies depending on how many books are bought (n).

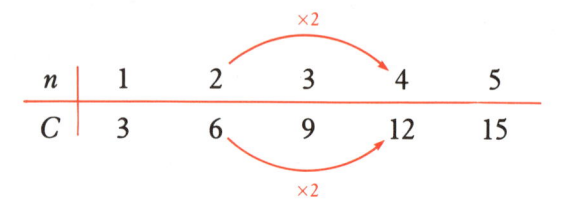

n	1	2	3	4	5
C	3	6	9	12	15

As the number of books increases, the cost increases by the same proportion. We call this **direct proportionality**, or **direct variation**, and we write

$C \propto n$

For each pair of values in the table, $\dfrac{C}{n} = 3$. We call this number the **constant of variation**, and usually denote it by the letter k.

We can use this constant to work out an equation linking C and n, and the cost of any number of books.

In this example | | **In general**

$C \propto n$ ← Write down the statement of variation. → $C \propto n$

$k = \dfrac{C}{n} = 3$ ← Work out the constant of variation. → $k = \dfrac{C}{n}$

$C = 3n$ ← Write down the equation which connects C and n. → $C = kn$

32 books cost £96. | | x books cost £kx.

When we plot the points from the table onto a graph, we get a straight line which passes through the origin.

This is always true for direct variation.

We say this is the graph of (number, cost).

Here are some examples for you to try.

A1 Julie is driving along at a constant speed. The distance (d km) she has travelled varies directly as the time (t hours) she has been driving.

After two hours she has travelled 210 km.

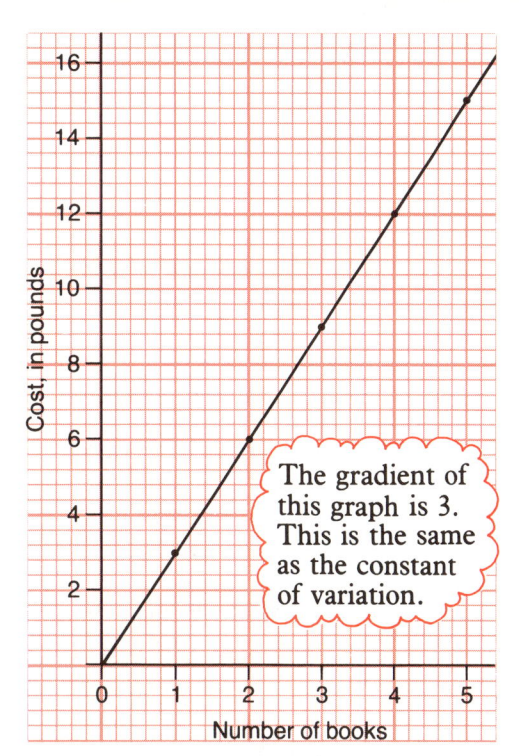

The gradient of this graph is 3. This is the same as the constant of variation.

(a) Write this information as a statement of variation.

(b) Calculate the constant of variation.

(c) Write down a formula connecting d and t.

(d) How far does she travel in 45 minutes?

(e) What happens to d when the time is halved?

(f) Sketch the graph of (time, distance).

A2 The circumference (C cm) of a circle varies directly as the radius (r cm). A circle of radius 10 cm has circumference 20π cm.

(a) Write this information as a statement of variation.

(b) Calculate the circumference of a circle with radius 6·5 cm.

(c) Calculate the radius of a circle with circumference $3·5\pi$ cm.

(d) What happens to the circumference when the radius is doubled?

(e) What happens to the radius when the circumference is halved?

(f) Sketch the graph of (radius, circumference).

A3 The perimeter (P cm) of a regular pentagon varies directly as the length of its side (l cm).

(a) Calculate the constant of variation.

(b) Write down an equation connecting P and l.

(c) What happens to P when l is reduced by 25%?

(d) What happens to l if P is reduced by 20%?

(e) Sketch the graph of (l, P).

A4 Ohm's law states that if a voltage (V volts) is applied across an electrical component in which a current of I amperes is flowing, then $I \propto V$.

For one component it is found that when V is 30 V, I is 5 A.

(a) Calculate the constant of variation, and write down an equation connecting I and V.

(b) Calculate (i) I when V is 0·3 V
(ii) V when I is 1·25 A

B More interesting direct variation

Carpet is sold by the square metre, with each square metre costing £10. This table shows how the cost of carpeting a square room varies depending on the size of the room.

Length of wall l m	1	2	3	4
Area of room l^2 m²	1	4	9	16
Cost of carpet £C	10	40	90	160

Here the relationship is between the area and the cost, not between the length and the cost.

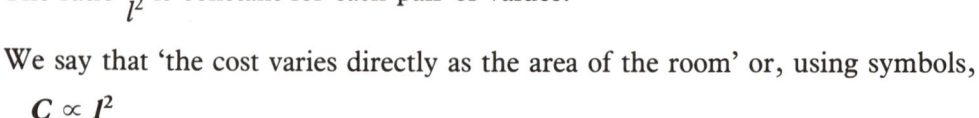

The ratio $\frac{C}{l^2}$ is constant for each pair of values.

We say that 'the cost varies directly as the area of the room' or, using symbols,

$$C \propto l^2$$

As before, we can find the constant of variation and an equation connecting C and l.

In this example	**In general**
$C \propto l^2$	$C \propto l^2$
$k = \dfrac{C}{l^2} = 10$	$k = \dfrac{C}{l^2}$
$C = 10\, l^2$	$C = kl^2$

When we draw the graph of (area of room, cost), we again get a straight line passing through the origin.

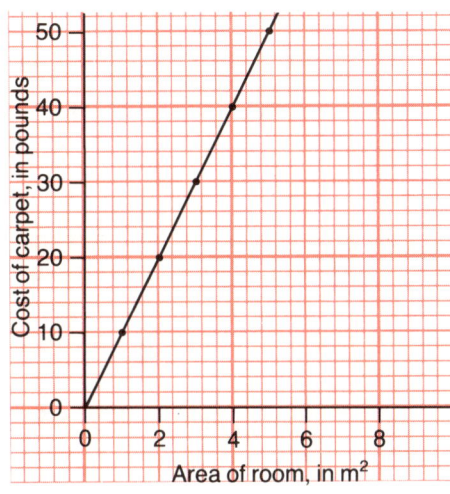

Here are some examples for you to try.

B1 Radbury's makes square bars of chocolate in different sizes (of side l cm). All the bars are the same thickness, so the weight (w grams) of each bar varies directly as the area of the top of the bar.

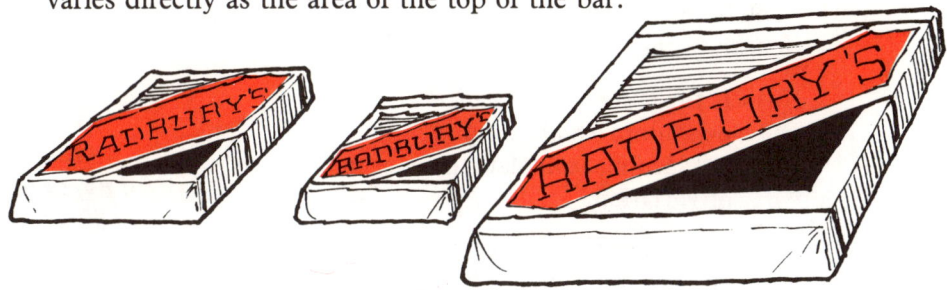

(a) Complete this table of values.

Length of side	l cm	1	2	3	4	...	10
Area of top	l^2 cm²	1	4				
Weight	w g	20		180			

(b) Write the information as a statement of variation, and calculate the constant of variation.

(c) Write down an equation connecting w and l.

(d) Calculate the weight of a bar of chocolate with side 12 cm.

(e) Calculate the length of a bar of chocolate with weight 320 g.

(f) If the side is doubled in length, what happens to the weight?

(g) Sketch the graph of (area of top, weight).

B2 The surface area of a sphere varies directly as the square of its diameter.

(a) The diameter of a golf ball is approximately half that of a tennis ball.

If the surface area of a golf ball is approximately 50 cm², calculate the approximate surface area of a tennis ball.

(b) If the surface area of a football is 64 times that of a golf ball, how many times bigger is the radius of a football than the radius of a golf ball?

B3 The volume of a cube (V cm³) varies as the cube of the length of its side (l cm).

(a) How many times bigger in volume is a cube of length 5 cm than a cube of length 2 cm?

(b) How many times bigger in length is a cube of volume 1728 cm³ than a cube of side 3 cm?

(c) What happens to the volume of a cube if its length is decreased by 25%?

B4 The time of a pendulum's swing (T seconds) varies as the square root of its length (l cm).

(a) If the time of swing of a pendulum 16 cm long is 0·8 seconds, calculate the constant of variation.

(b) If a pendulum has to have a one-second swing, what length should it be?

(c) A grandfather clock has a pendulum 64 cm long. By how much must the pendulum be lengthened if its time of swing has to be increased by 25%?

C Inverse variation

Jill is making a journey of 100 km. The time she takes to complete the journey varies depending on her average speed.

This is shown in the table below.

	speed increases →			
Speed s km/h	10	20	50	100
Time t hours	10	5	2	1
	← time decreases			

When we draw the graph of (speed, time), it looks like this.

This shape is called a **rectangular hyperbola**. All the variation graphs we have met so far have been straight lines through the origin, so it is not true to say that $t \propto s$.

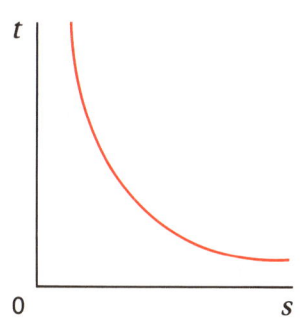

Let's look for another relationship.

Speed s km/h	10	20	50	100
$\dfrac{1}{\text{Speed}}$	0·1	0·05	0·02	0·01
Time t hours	10	5	2	1

When we draw the graph of $(\dfrac{1}{\text{speed}}, \text{time})$, we find it looks like this.

This is a straight line through the origin, like all the other variation graphs we have met.

We can say that 't varies directly as $\dfrac{1}{s}$' or that 't varies **inversely** as s', and we write

$$t \propto \dfrac{1}{s}$$

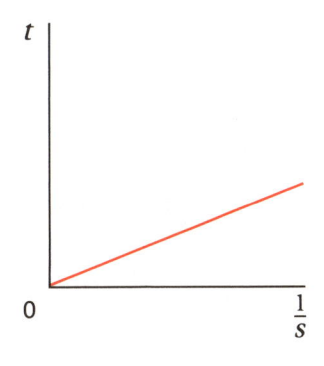

135

Now let's look for the constant of variation.

Speed	10	20	50	100
$\dfrac{1}{\text{Speed}}$	0·1	0·05	0·02	0·01
Time	10	5	2	1
Time ÷ $\dfrac{1}{\text{Speed}}$	100	100	100	100

$t \div \dfrac{1}{s} = t \times \dfrac{s}{1}$
$= ts$

$k = 100$

As before, we can use this constant to write down an equation connecting s and t.

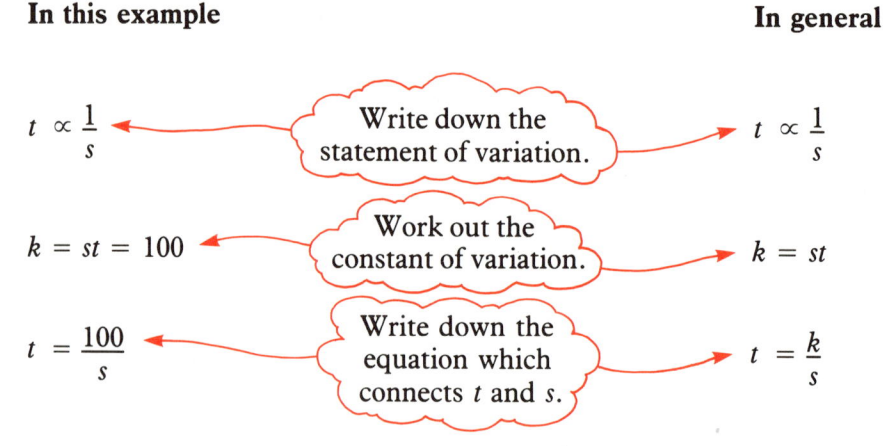

In this example   **In general**

$t \propto \dfrac{1}{s}$ ← Write down the statement of variation. → $t \propto \dfrac{1}{s}$

$k = st = 100$ ← Work out the constant of variation. → $k = st$

$t = \dfrac{100}{s}$ ← Write down the equation which connects t and s. → $t = \dfrac{k}{s}$

Here are some examples for you to try.

C1 X and Y are two variables such that $X \propto \dfrac{1}{Y}$. Y is 5·2 when X is 14·9.

(a) Calculate the constant of variation and write down an equation connecting X and Y.

(b) Work out Y when X is 8.

(c) Sketch the graph of $(\dfrac{1}{X}, Y)$.

C2   Variable a varies inversely as variable b.

(a) Calculate the constant of variation and fill in the missing values in this table.

a	2	3	4	5
b	1·5	1		0·5

(b) What happens to b when a is multiplied by 3?

(c) What happens to a when b is reduced by $\frac{1}{2}$?

(d) Sketch the graph of $(\frac{1}{a}, b)$.

C3 The wavelength (w m) of a radio wave varies inversely as the frequency (f kHz). The wavelength of West Sound is 290 m, and its frequency is 1035 kHz. (1 kHz = 1000 Hz.)

(a) Calculate the constant of variation, to one significant figure.

(b) These diagrams show the positions of various radio stations on radio dials.

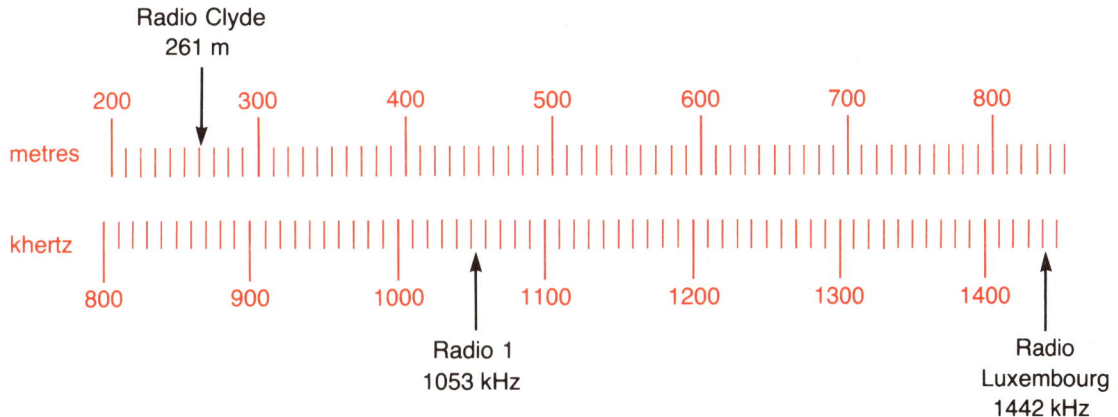

Complete this table, making all calculations to the nearest unit.

Radio station	Wavelength, in m	Frequency, in kHz
Radio Clyde	261	
Radio 1		1053
Radio Luxembourg		1442

(c) Radio 2 can be found in two places. One has frequency 693 kHz and the other has frequency 909 kHz.

Which of these two positions has the longer wavelength, and by how much?

(d) Radio 1 can be found on 275 m and 285 m. By what percentage is the frequency at the 275 m position higher?

C4 The cost of a coach outing (£C) varies inversely as the number of people who go (n). If 42 people go, the cost will be £2·50 each.

(a) The cost increased to £3 because some people could not go. How many people did not attend?

(b) The organising committee wants to reduce the cost to £2 each. What is the minimum number of people who must go on the trip to make this reduction possible?

(c) Each coach holds 54 people. If 70 people want to attend, calculate the cost per person.

(d) On 2 mm graph paper, draw an accurate graph to show the cost per person for any number of people between 40 and 80.

(e) From the graph, estimate how many people should go for the cost per person to be the cheapest.

D More interesting inverse variation

We can work out the volume of a pyramid using the formula

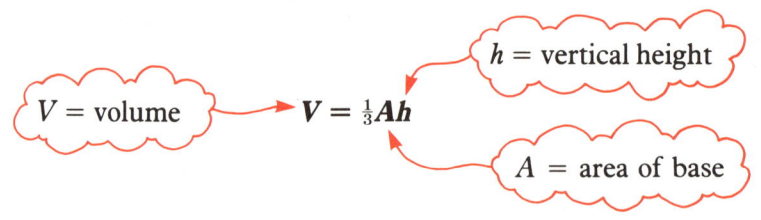

V = volume $V = \frac{1}{3}Ah$ h = vertical height A = area of base

D1 These square-based pyramids all have the same volume.

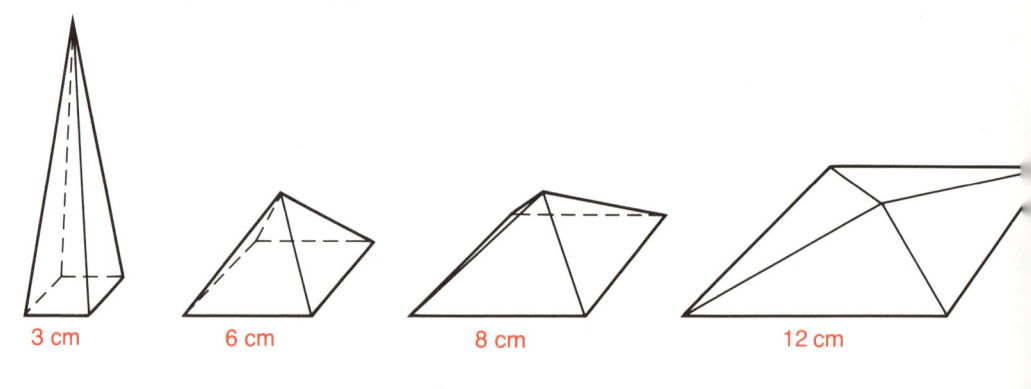

3 cm   6 cm   8 cm   12 cm

(a) Copy and complete this table for the pyramids.

Length of base	l cm	3	6	8	12
Area of base	l^2 cm²				
Height	h cm³				
Volume	V cm³	120	120	120	120

(b) Sketch the graphs of $(\frac{1}{l}, h)$ and $(\frac{1}{l^2}, h)$.

(c) Which of the following statements is true: $h \propto \frac{1}{l}$ or $h \propto \frac{1}{l^2}$?

(d) Calculate the constant of variation.

(e) Calculate the height of the pyramid of base length 4 cm and volume 120 cm³.

(f) What happens to the height when the length of the base is doubled?

D2 A cone is a pyramid with a circular base.

These cones all have the same volume.

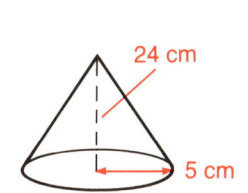

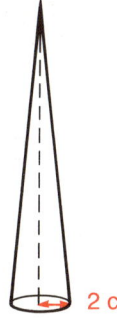

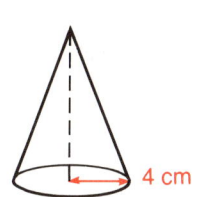

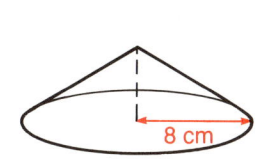

(a) The first cone has base radius 5 cm and height 24 cm. Calculate the volume of the cone.

(b) In the same way as in question D1, show that $h \propto \frac{1}{r^2}$.

(c) Calculate the constant of variation.

(d) What happens to the height when the radius is quartered?

D3 x and y are two variables such that $y \propto \frac{1}{\sqrt{x}}$, and y is 5 when x is 9.

(a) Find y when x is 25.

(b) Find x when y is 30.

D4 A varies inversely as the cube of b, and b is 2 when A is 0·4.

(a) Work out an equation connecting A and b.

(b) What happens to A if b is doubled?

D5 λ varies inversely as the square of θ.

Work out what happens to λ when θ is

(a) halved (b) doubled (c) reduced by 25%

Expressions such as $y \propto \frac{1}{x^2}$ and $a \propto \frac{1}{b^2}$ are known as **inverse square laws** and occur quite frequently in science. Here is another example using an inverse square law.

D6 A spacecraft is pulled towards the Earth by the force of gravity. The strength of the force depends on the distance of the object from the centre of the Earth. If F is the force of gravity and d km is the distance from the centre of the Earth, then it is known that $F \propto \frac{1}{d^2}$.

(a) The Earth has a radius of 6400 km. What fraction of the force of gravity at the Earth's surface would operate on a spacecraft 3200 km above the Earth's surface?

(b) How far above the surface of the Earth is an object on which the force of gravity is one-quarter that on the Earth's surface?

E A variation on variation

Here is a summary of the work on direct and inverse variation so far.

	Direct variation	Inverse variation
Statement of variation	$y \propto x$	$y \propto \frac{1}{x}$
Constant of variation	$k = \frac{y}{x}$	$k = xy$
Graph	y vs x (straight line through origin)	y vs $\frac{1}{x}$ (straight line through origin)

We can use these properties to work out whether a given set of data shows direct or inverse variation.

Worked example

Find out whether the following set of data shows direct or inverse variation, and calculate the constant of variation.

p	3	4	12	8	6
q	16	12	4	6	8

If direct variation, $\frac{q}{p}$ will be constant.

p	3	4	12	8	6
q	16	12	4	6	8
$\frac{q}{p}$	$5\frac{1}{3}$	3	$\frac{1}{3}$	$\frac{3}{4}$	$1\frac{1}{2}$

Not direct variation!

If inverse variation, pq will be constant.

p	3	4	12	8	6
q	16	12	4	6	8
pq	48	48	48	48	48

This is inverse variation, and $k = 48$

E1 Find out whether each of these sets of data shows direct or inverse variation, and calculate the constant of variation.

(a)
s	4	5	6	7	8
C	20	25	30	35	40

(b)
x	2	3	6	9	36
y	9	6	3	2	0·5

(c)
a	0·8	1·6	3·2
B	8	4	2

(d)
y	0·1	0·2	0·3
z	50	100	150

Sometimes the variation is a bit more complicated.

It might take the form $y \propto x^2$, or $a \propto \dfrac{1}{\sqrt{b}}$, for example.

E2 One of the following types of relationship holds for each of the sets of data in this question.

$$y \propto x^2 \qquad y \propto \dfrac{1}{\sqrt{x}} \qquad y \propto \sqrt{x} \qquad y \propto \dfrac{1}{x^2}$$

Work out which of the relationships holds for each set of data, and sketch its graph.

The first one has been done as an example.

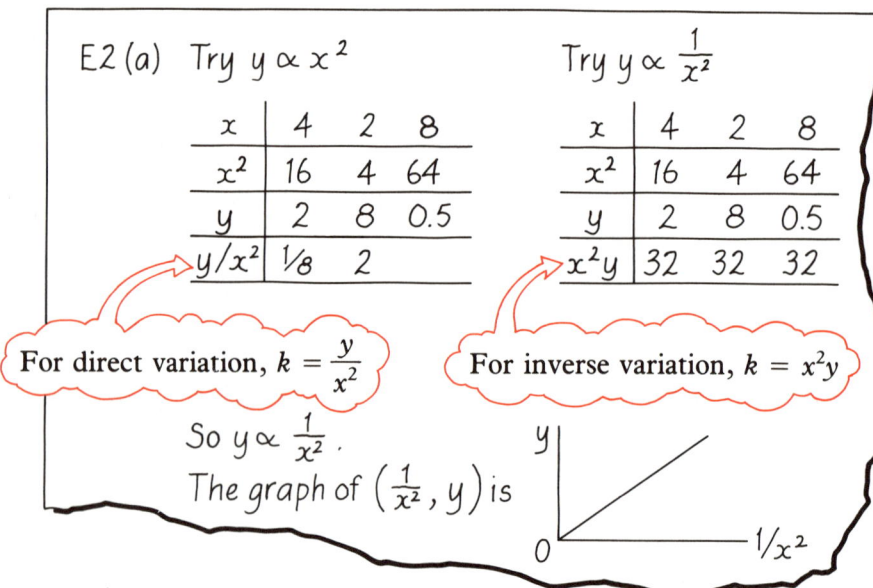

(a)

x	4	2	8
y	2	8	0·5

E2 (a) Try $y \propto x^2$

x	4	2	8
x^2	16	4	64
y	2	8	0.5
y/x^2	1/8	2	

For direct variation, $k = \dfrac{y}{x^2}$

Try $y \propto \dfrac{1}{x^2}$

x	4	2	8
x^2	16	4	64
y	2	8	0.5
$x^2 y$	32	32	32

For inverse variation, $k = x^2 y$

So $y \propto \dfrac{1}{x^2}$.

The graph of $\left(\dfrac{1}{x^2}, y\right)$ is

(b)

x	4	16	9	25
y	32	64	48	80

(c)

x	9	16	25	36
y	30	40	50	60

(d)

x	2	3	4	5
y	2	4·5	8	12·5

(e)

x	0·1	0·2	0·3	0·4
y	360	90	40	22·5

F Joint variation

F1 Look at these cuboids.

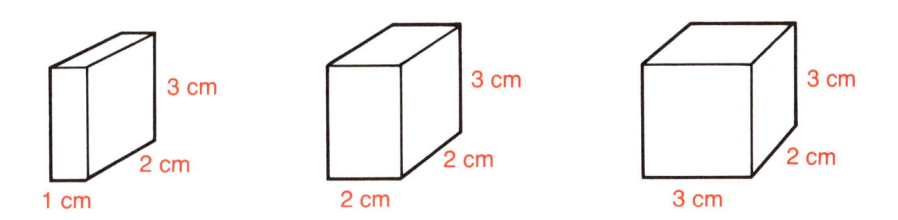

The breadths and heights remain the same, but the lengths vary.

(a) Copy and complete this table for the cuboids.

(h = height, b = breadth, l = length and V = volume.)

(b) Sketch the graph of (l, V).

(c) Write down a statement of variation.

bh	6	6	
l	1		3
V	6		

F2 Look at these cuboids.

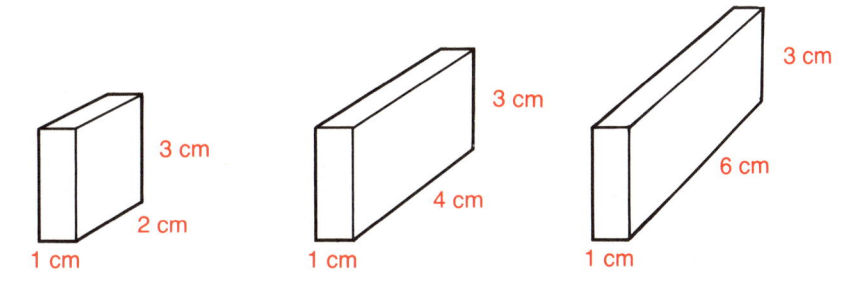

The lengths and heights remain the same, but the breadths vary.

(a) Copy and complete this table for these cuboids.

(b) Sketch the graph of (b, V).

lh	3		
b		4	6
V			

(c) Write down a statement of variation and calculate its constant.

F3 Look at these cuboids.

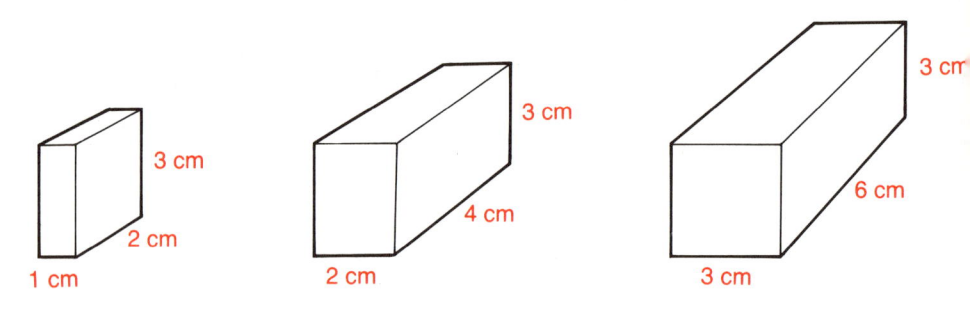

This time the height remains the same, but the lengths *and* the breadths vary.

(a) Copy and complete this table for these cuboids.

(b) Sketch the graphs of (l, V), (b, V) and (lb, V).

(c) Write down a true statement of variation, and calculate the constant.

l	1		3
b	2	4	
h	3		
lb	2		
V	6		

In general, when the volume varies depending on the length *and* the breadth, we say that 'V varies as l and b'. This is called **joint variation**, and we write

$$V \propto lb$$

As with the other forms of variation, we can work out a constant of variation and write an equation.

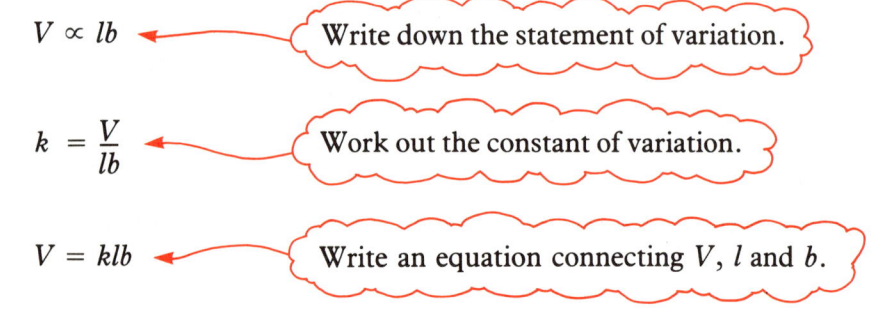

$V \propto lb$ ← Write down the statement of variation.

$k = \dfrac{V}{lb}$ ← Work out the constant of variation.

$V = klb$ ← Write an equation connecting V, l and b.

Here are some examples for you to try.

F4 (a) If the cuboids in question F3 had height 2 cm, calculate the constant of variation.

(b) Write down an equation connecting V, l and b.

(c) Calculate the volume if $l = 4$ cm and $b = 6$ cm.

(d) What happens to the volume if the length is doubled?

F5 X varies jointly as Y and Z.
X is 6 when Y is 2 and Z is 1.

(a) Calculate the constant of variation and write down an equation connecting X, Y and Z.

(b) Calculate Z if $X = 3·3$ and $Y = 1·1$.

(c) What happens to X if Y is multiplied by 3 and Z is halved?

F6 A varies as B and inversely as C.
A is 3 when B is 12 and C is 6.

(a) Calculate the constant of variation and write down an equation connecting A, B and C.

(b) What happens to A if B is doubled and C is halved?

F7 The volume of a cylinder (V cm^3) varies as the square of its radius (r cm) and as its height (h cm).

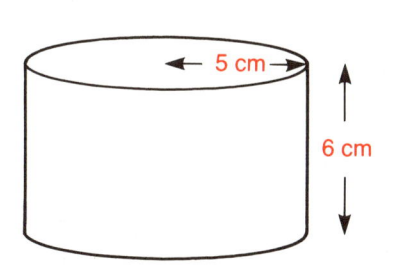

The volume of this cylinder is 150π.

(a) Calculate the constant of variation.

(b) What happens to the volume when
   (i) the height is doubled
   (ii) the radius is halved

F8 p varies directly as q and inversely as r.

(a) What happens to p when r is trebled?

(b) What is the percentage change in p if q is halved?

F9 a varies directly as b and c.

(a) If b is doubled and c is halved, what happens to a?

(b) If b is increased by 50% and c is decreased by 75%, what is the percentage change in a?

G A variety of variation

G1 The speed of a journey varies inversely as the time taken. Work out the percentage change in speed (faster or slower) if the time is

(a) decreased by 50%   (b) increased by 25%

G2 If $Y \propto \dfrac{1}{X}$ and X is multiplied by $\tfrac{2}{7}$, what happens to Y?

G3 The surface area of a sphere varies as the square of its diameter.

The diameter of the Moon is half that of Mars and the Moon's surface area is 3.8×10^7 km².

Calculate the surface area of Mars.

G4 The volume of a sphere varies as the cube of its diameter.

If the diameter of a spherical balloon is increased from 15 cm to 25 cm, calculate the percentage increase in the balloon's volume.

G5 If $A \propto \dfrac{1}{B^2}$, work out the percentage change in A if B is increased by 30%.

G6 The resistance of a wire varies directly as its length and inversely as the square of its radius.

If the resistance is 10 units when the length is 100 m and the radius is 0·4 cm, find what length of the same wire would give a resistance of 20 units.

Consolidation 3

The cosine rule

1. Calculate all the angles of a triangle with sides 4 cm, 7 cm and 9 cm.

2. Calculate the length of the unknown side of triangle ABC, in which BC = 9 cm, AC = 11 cm and $\hat{C} = 88°$.

3. Calculate all the sides and angles of triangle XYZ, in which $\hat{X} = 72°$, YZ = 5 cm and XY = 8 cm.

4. Two of the sides of a triangular field measure 150 m and 175 m, and the angle between them is 132°.

   Calculate the total length of fencing the farmer will need to go right round the field if there is a gate 2 m wide in one of the sides.

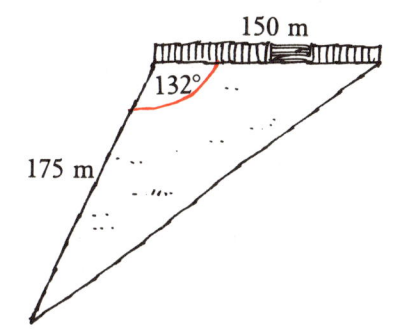

5. An inn sign is to be hung from a bracket made from strips of metal with lengths as shown.

   Calculate the largest of the angles marked.

Loans and insurance

1. One year, the insurance premium for a Ford Fiesta is £240. If the annual premium increases by 8% the next year, calculate how much a motorist with 40% no claims discount would have to pay.

2. Jenny pays an insurance premium of £120 for her motorcycle.
   (a) After one year's safe motoring she earns a 10% no claims discount. Calculate her next year's premium.
   (b) If, during the next year, premiums rise by 9·5% and Jenny's no claims discount rises to 15%, how much will she pay?

3. Robert's house is valued at £47 500 and its contents at £18 000.
   If he takes out insurance with a company which charges 11p per £100 for buildings and 23·3p per £100 for contents, calculate Robert's total premium for his house and its contents.

4. Why do you think that insurance companies charge higher premiums for houses in the city than for houses in the country?

5. Nelly has taken out a loan with her bank for £700 to pay for a holiday abroad. She must pay the loan back over two years at an interest rate of 9·5% per annum.

   If she makes 24 equal payments, work out how much she pays each month.

6. Flash Cash will lend money to anybody for anything – at a price! They charge an annual interest rate of 39·4%.

   John takes out a loan with them for £1500 to finance a new business. He undertakes to repay the loan in equal monthly payments over five years.

   Calculate the cost of each monthly payment.

Patterns

1. Write down the next-term rule for each of the following sequences.
   (a) 2, 4, 6, 8, 10, . . .
   (b) 100, 95, 90, . . .
   (c) 0·1, 0·2, 0·3, . . .
   (d) 3, 9, 27, 81, . . .

2. Work out a rule for finding the nth term of each of the following sequences.

   (a)
Position	1	2	3	4	. . . n
Term	2	4	6	8	. . .

   (b)
Position	1	2	3	4	. . . n
Term	0·1	0·2	0·3	0·4	. . .

   (c)
Position	1	2	3	4	. . . n
Term	3	9	27	81	. . .

   (d)
Position	1	2	3	4	. . . n
Term	4	9	14	19	. . .

3   Here is the any-term rule for a sequence: $u_n = -3n + 7$

(a) Calculate u_5, u_9 and u_{32}.

(b) Which term of the sequence has the value −23?

4   If $u_n = 2n^2 + 2$, write down the first four terms of the sequence.

Variation

1   $x \propto y^2$, and x is 105·5 when y is 5.

Calculate x when y is doubled.

2   The density of a gas varies inversely as its volume.
When the volume is 1·2 m³, the density is 2·8 kg/m³.

(a) Calculate the constant of variation.

(b) Calculate the volume when the density is increased by $\frac{1}{4}$.

3   p varies as q and as the square root of r.

What happens to p when q is halved and r is multiplied by 4?

4   a varies directly as b and inversely as c.
a is 40 when b is 20 and c is 10.

(a) Work out an equation connecting a, b and c.

(b) What happens to a when b is increased by 25% and c is halved?

5   Water is flowing into a tank of depth 60 cm at a steady rate. The depth of water in the tank varies as the square root of the time that the water has been flowing.

After nine minutes, the depth of water in the tank is 12 cm.

How long, to the nearest minute, would it take the tank to fill to the top?

6   The square of the time (in days) of a planet's revolution round the Sun varies as the cube of its distance from the Sun.

The Earth is $9·125 \times 10^7$ miles from the Sun and takes 365 days for one revolution.

Venus is $6·6 \times 10^7$ miles from the Sun.

Work out how long Venus takes to complete one revolution.